Microsoft Mon Amour

Hilarius Hofstede

Microsoft Mon Amour

7744 Lines To Disconnect From The Internet

USA Edition

Zip Records
MMXVII

For Laure

Introduction

In *Microsoft Mon Amour* Hilarius Hofstede engages in an outrageously witty battle against the erosion of language and the imagination caused by the overwhelming stream of information that is served to us via the screens of our computers and digital devices on a daily basis.

In 7.744 lines that take on the shape of a mysterious wave-like graph seemingly generated by a computer run amok, technology comes to clash with nature, online madness with offline boredom, psychiatric drugs with stone age rituals, and popstars with bisons; flint axes are wielded against the personal space program of Jeff Bezos, mammoth bones threaten Donald Trump's comb-over and Hillary Clinton disappears down the robot-hole.

If at first glance this text may look like some overelaborate practical joke or the nonsensical product of a deranged Silicon Valley copywriter tripping on one too many microdoses of LSD, it is worth calling to mind the long tradition of literary experimentation in which it can be situated; a tradition stretching back to at least Medieval times and the Hebrew practice of Melitzah, whereby quotations from religious scripture were rearranged and strung together to extract novel meaning from the source texts. Closer to our own time however, the obvious parallel is of course that of the cut-up technique, which – although often attributed to William Burroughs – was first widely employed by the Dadaists in the years around WWI. The Romanian Dadaist Tristan Tzara in fact gave the exact recipe for the cut-up in his 1920 "How to Make a Dadaist Poem": 'Take a newspaper. Take a pair of scissors' ...

Hofstede derives his material not from one but from a vast array of sources: pop and funk lyrics, political one-liners and advertising slogans, philosophical aphorisms, psychiatric jargon, techno babble and social media speak are all treated as raw ingredients for his linguistic supercollage. Moreover, his manipulation of this source material does not limit itself to 'cutting and pasting' but includes making changes to the individual elements themselves as well as the introduction of words and phrases altogether of his own invention.

Likewise the typographical aspect of the text, far from being a gimmick, serves to reinforce the author's intention. Again, the influence of early twentieth-century literary modernism is evident: the origins of the arrangement of the lines into their distinct graph-like pattern can easily be traced back to the experiments with visual poetry conducted by Apollinaire or the rhythmical typography of the Flemish poet Paul van Ostaijen. Apollinaire would describe the typographical innovation of his collection *Caligrammes* (1918) as signaling the 'brilliant end of typography at the dawn of the new means of reproduction that are the cinema and the phonograph.' It seems obvious that by inventing his own typographical conventions in response to the advent of the ultimate means of reproduction that is the internet, Hofstede firmly positions himself within this tradition. By molding his lines into a highly ordered, apparently computer-generated shape he visually reinforces both the theme of the artificiality of language in the digital age and the artificial nature of his own text.

What Hofstede presents us with is his own 'Meanderthal', combining the Dutch word for language, 'taal', with 'meander' and 'Neanderthal': a language that associatively jumps and zigzags through time and space, joining one fragment of meaning to another. This radical form of intertextual sampling requires readers to actively participate in the generation of meaning. And this truly pays off: simply turning on, tuning in and surfing the wave of endless punning and free association will almost instantaneously produce a mild psychedelic effect.

If *Microsoft Mon Amour* can be read as one long interior monologue, then whose thought process are we listening to? A poetic hacker on the digital garbage belt, a post-diluvian alchemist of language? We are informed that the speaker has 'lost his memory card' and 'survives on bison livers in the world of the Deepnet', his head resounding with a chorus of voices never ceasing to remind him to check his order status, consider trending topics, add native American spears to his basket on eBay and read up on the latest celebrity fun facts.

The key to unlock this esoteric pattern of associations can be found in Hofstede's artistic credo 'Paleo Psycho Pop' (or simply 'PPP'), which sums up his desire to 'open up an ancient bewilderment, a savage nature in everyday pop things'. Hofstede's aim is none other than the creation of a new form of popular art by 'reaching back to the Paleolithic times, those of the very first human image making', not in the literal sense but 'through the stages of the mind'.* The image on the cover of the present publication, a traditional tiki tattoo as worn by Polynesian warriors transformed into a smiley, gives expression to this same principle.

The problem occupying the speaker's mind is that 'online is never off the record' because 'the internet is a global voyeuristic disorder'. He resides on the 'dark side of the phone' suffering from 'weak web presence' and 'online isolation', but he has 'diamonds on the inside of his skull'.

---

* For more information on Hofstede's earlier publications and his work as an artist see www.hilariushofstede.com

Throughout the text, the fundamental real-life values love, nature and creativity are contrasted with their evil twins in virtual reality: porn, advertising and general media-induced hypnosis. 'I'm havin' a real real-world problem here', the voice insists: 'Tristan did not meet Isolde on the internet.'

Remembering our offline existence, the speaker 'scrolls down memory lane', looking at 'Polaroids of a fading world'. They depict scenes as good as forgotten yet strangely familiar: a long expected love letter at the doormat, a typewriter that sounds 'like Mozart', the image of a handshake or someone using a fax machine. The contours of a non-linear story gradually emerge: 'In the beginning there was Microsoft Word', but now we are lost inside the 'Rock n' Roll Hell of Fame' where the only law is 'an eye for an iPhone, a tooth for a Bluetooth'. In this 'digital dark age' the voice longs back to a time when it was still possible 'not to know what time it was' while simultaneously dreaming up a new aeon to come, that of 'paleopsychoanalysis' and 'prehistoric pop-art', of e-security obliterated by volcanic ash.

The planet is suffering from a 'New World Disorder' where creatures wearing 'Trump mask replicas' or shapeshifting into the hideous hologrammic representations of Bill O'Reilly and Alex Jones are given free rein to poison the minds of an already brainwashed audience with populist drivel and distorted propaganda. A sinister figure slithers 'into the White House through the bathroom window', while Europe recoils into xenophobia and sells out its once sacred ideals: it's 'Grexit through the EU giftshop'!

As he climbs the 'Internet Mountain', the speaker – this postmodern Paleo warrior – is engaged in an unrelenting battle against 'Barbara bushmen' and the zombies of Silicon Valley, like a new Sisyphus. For the enemy is legion, encompassing the entire pandemonium of pop and celebrity presided over by the grotesque figure of 'Bono Christ'. A veritable 'orgy of names' leaves the reader's head ringing: Lady Gaga, Miley Cyrus, Paris Hilton, Britney Spears, Bill Gates, Elon Musk, Steve Jobs, Tim Cook, Kim Kardashian, Caitlyn Jenner, Simon Cowell, and so on and so forth, *ad infinitum*. Striding on the side of the protagonist we find an imaginary army of 'shamanic schizophrenics' that includes the funk warriors George Clinton, Bootsy Collins, James Brown, Prince, and of course Joe Bowie of legendary N.Y. funk outfit Defunkt, for whose forthcoming album *Mastervolt* Hofstede recently composed the lyrics. Together this merry band of holy pranksters forms a chorus forever jamming 'on the one' in order to remind mankind of the fact that 'once there were more bisons than gigabytes'.

Uncompromising and bitingly satirical, *Microsoft Mon Amour* at once exposes the abyss of meaninglessness beneath today's digital 'newspeak' and manages to regain some of the magic that language has been robbed of. A work of daring literary innovation, Hofstede's commentary on the age of virtual reality reveals all the traits of composition by a discerning human mind, a human eye and a human hand, pointing the reader to a way out of the dark labyrinth of the web in search of a dazzling screenless dawn somewhere in an offline land ...

G.H. van Koningsveld

Microsoft Mon Amour

You can log out anytime but you can never leave.

53206.

Dot con.

Lost ideals.

ShrinkedIn.

Walk The Talk.

Asking myselfie.

A screen is a wall.

The Origin of PC's.

The War on Tourism.

Dark side of the phone.

Papua New Hampshire.

Make The Rich History.

Emojinal, very emojinal...

Climbing Mount Internet.

Nature versus Technology.

We can't, therefore we are.

Gentlemen Take Polaroids.

Heaven is God's Homepage.

Ashes to ashes, DOS to DOS.

The Magical Microsoft Tour.

Breakfast at Connectiffany's.

The Internet is full. Go away.

Raging Against The Machine.

Buffalo Bill Gates: WiFi Cody.

The best things in Life are real.

Waiting on the world to change.

What dots around, coms around.

Online mania, offline depression.

(Welcome to) Stone Age America.

Halliburton... knows how to party.

We buy too much, and think too little.

The only way out is the way straight in!

Mass distraction from elite domination.

Under The Bridge Over Troubled Water.

The Internet is the Esperanto of Despair.

Digital baptism for those who fear water.

I am just a cowboy, lonesome on the trail.

The sleep of Reason produces computers.

Tom Cruzzi's home-baking beats all, folks.

The new Batman: Hillary Gotham Clinton.

The Micky Mausoleum of American Liberty.

Luckily only 9% of the world population is white.

Sir Hillary climbing the Shimalaya for President!

Never was so much taken from so many by so few.

One World. One Bank. One Account. All of Google.

Microsoft Mon Amour is waiting to take you away.

The George Clinton Clinic of Funkforward Recovery.

Donald Trump & 3rdEyeGirl: She's always in my hair...

The Cumshots of Commerce are the Confetti of Capital.

Preemptive MacBook Airstrikes against the Middle-East.

When sharks talk to dolphins, jellyfish are the translators.

Memory is drinking water from the ocean with two hands.

Oh, yeah, well, alright, we're Jebbin', I want to Jeb it with you.

By the type of religious experience that Dionysos inaugurates.

A long, long, long, long time ago, before the wind before the snow.

The sun, the darkness, the winds are all listening to what we now say.

Rowing the speedboat of Information Technology into the Abyss of Folly.

'Microsoft Mon Amour is a rightly detailed and compelling read.' L.A. Times.

Fiat Lux.

Rising Son.

Sacred land.

Modern Tides.

Back to bisons.

Catching robots.

Que Viva Mexico!

Fight for your mind.

Zippin' up my boots.

Man versus Machine.

New World Monkeys.

Planet of the Trumps.

Heinz Across America.

The Eagle Has Landed.

A. Hinkel: Mein Trumpf.

Im Westen nichts Neues.

Connected to what exactly?

Not to know what time it is.

Where Do The Children Play?

www.... coming out of my nose.

Pantha Rei (all but the Internet).

I'm dreaming of you, mon amour.

Introducing... Dr. Trump-N-Furter.

India Arie: I Am Light, I Am Light...

The rocky horror... the rocky horror...

The screen is your only mirror today.

Sarah Palin's Mad Hatter's Tea Party.

Dying and rising, but rising once again.

Habsburgers, McMenus and PC-dinners.

Portrait of Andy Trump as Donald Warhol.

The Internet is an asylum with many gates.

Throwing Melania Trump at the kitchen sink.

I've been riding this tiger for quite some time.

Autumn leaves don't tell no tales of tomorrow.

She was the Venus of Milo in her sister's jeans?

Insanely Gifted: The Life and Times of Eminem.

Volare...

Sleep on it.

I Can't Breathe.

Sea of Madness.

Hey ho! Let's go!

Account Dracula.

Blax Panther Rex.

A PC never smiles.

Jovem Negro Vivo.

The eye is the limit.

Going underground.

Too Bush To Be True.

Empty sea, full world.

Disconnecting people.

Out of Date and Time.

Egos never really land.

Prince: Family Name...

Thou Shalt Not Google.

Donald Duck or die 2018.

Our disconnected hearts.

Consume, donate, forget.

Saving lives sells records.

Truman Don't Kill Capotes.
We're Back In The U.S.S.A.!
Google: Search and Destroy.
Terms of use, terms of abuse.
Online is never off the record.
Rachid Taha: Rock El Casbah.
I know we've come a long way.
Grexit through the EU Gift shop.
Speed is the enemy of the angels.
Hi Justin, I'm a Mexican belieber!
My hair does not get great reviews.
Laughing all the way to the Banksy.
When Bill Gates roars his ugly head.
Download The New Oval Office 2018.
Questlove as Black House Spokesman.
The day the world did not explode, yes?
You can't say no to the Bootsy & the Bass!
Miss Information vs. Miss Communication.
Waiting on the world to change the world, yes!
D'Angelo in charge of Homeland Funk Security.
They don't know what you know, how could they?
Of firewire, pop-up help and frozen mammoth bones.
Caramel, bonbons et chocolat (parole, parole, parole!).
Eagles attacking drones, can't have enough of them yaw!
Cinema is not meant for the screen of a computer or your television.
Your personal computti blow the winds from all corners of the world.
Bow Wow Wow Yippee Yo Yippee Ye: Barking Mad (Wild In America).
Change Country.
Heaven Up Here.
RIP Eric Gardner.
Reality is different.
New World Disorder.
The Return of the Real.
Just let it all Trump out.
Warlike Times... War Times...
You say you want a revolution?
The chase is better than the catch.
What's App, Dr. Trump-N-Furter?
The only Bill I know is Bill Laswell.

I prefer to watch people passing by.

Shooting black kids is what they're at.

Be part of the next generation of Skype.

The Internet is a giant no smoking section.

Free your mind and your mouse will follow.

In the desert of Sudan and the gardens of Japan...

ColdFusion, MacBook Provo, Starbucks & Stripes.

www: Land without Evening and Land without Dawn.

I can't stand my brain against my window of the mind.

The Strawberry Smart Search Fields Forever Hearts Club Bandaman Vibrations.

Nothing is what it seems in New Orleans, or anywhere else in the US for that matter.

Cherry Colony: 1 0z. EFFEN BlackCherry White Vodka, Pepsi Cola, 1 0z. potassium alum.

Bridge...

Asocial media.

Young Americans.

Sign up to die now.

Drip drip drip drip.

iThink therefore iAm.

Only the Big Dream is left alive.

The Silicon Valley is NOT America.

Don't you miss it, don't you miss it.

Every growing boy needs a little joy.

Inside Paris Hilton's Million Dollar Closet.

Clear Your Mind And Your Love Will Follow.

Diving back into Pre-Columbian civilizations.

If you wanna go higher, then we gotta get deep!

Rockstars and politicians share high dentist bills.

The Global Tufted Capuchins Take-Over of Virtuality.

Jeb Bush: 'My father is the greatest man alive in my mind'.

You're not all on the same page, You Young American Droogies!

AXIOMERICA: Bill Laswell | Axiom Ambient – Lost In (The) Translation.

'Microsoft Mon Amour is a clear and riveting account of our world today.' Rolling Stone.

Hare Krishna.

Elonely Musk.

pRose-Buddha.

Guess you what!

Out Of The Dark.

Chelsea Mourning.

Copyright = Suicide.

New World, Old Sea.

Small world, Big lies.

Of dreams and drones.

Elvis has left the sauna.

Our shadows are burning.

Pink Trump, Punk Trump.

Thin Lizza Minelli: NY NY.

Turn your lights down low.

Sign in to continue to suffer.

Patriotic drinks you will love.

Loosing our Humanity again.

Daydreaming the night away.

I wanna be your monkey tree.

You look vintage all over, guy!

Water, drum, dream, birth, light.

That this world is going out of kilter.

Pop culture makes babies of all of us.

George Sand resting on Chopin's beach.

Am I watching Donald LSDuck, or what?

USA: I can't believe what my eyes are hearing!

Thin Lizza Milli Vanilla: Blame it on the (b)rain.

We really need music in politics, ladiesz & gentsz.

Hit me with your selfie-stick, hit me hit me hit me!

I. Arie: I am not the pieces of the dream I left behind.

Take a look at these hands, take a look at these hands!

It came into the White House through the bathroom window.

Erykah Badu as the first female black president, simply simple.

Excuse me, but you're interfering with my private space program.

The Vultures pull at my intestines, on top of the Internet Mountain.

Dino spermatozoa from the time we did not have to listen to D. Trump.

'Microsoft Mon Amour is a positive force in the world.' Noam Chomsky.

Let me sing my song each day. At the end of today, let my song tell people who I am.
Overkill.

My Wish List.

Sexy and I know it.

Innovation at work.

Zillatron: Fuzz Face!

Clear Human History.

The Desiring Machine.

Lizards and Live world.

Most porn is American.

Talking about a resolution...

I got weak web-presence doctor!

I've had sex with Ellen Degeneres.

Everybody has gone to the movies.

Native American Weapons for sale.

Netflixing you out of house and home.

Emancipate yourself from digital slavery.

Yelp, Bing, Yahoo, Apple, Google, Twitter.

Psychogenic vomiting of all things Internet.

Even Mitt Romney's potatoes are mormons.

Once there were more bisons than gigabytes.

Wifipedia, flint spearheads and Debt Slavery.

Why speed up life? There is so precious little of it.

The Fascists Coming Out Of The Bushes Worldwide.

The Darknet will one day burst with volcanic criminality.

The truth about hair and other Funkhansa Fire Journeys.

Remember, Back In The Day (The Best of Bootsy Collins).

That's how we know who we are. Our song tells us who we are.

Donny Trump & The Brides of Frank-N-Furter: Mucha Muchada!

Every download is now a movie we make for ourselves in our sleep.

Offline immanence or the introduction to the non-fascist way of life.

When the bison herds roamed America, computers were nonexistent.

Men's Pajamas, Hopi Bow Arrows Wall Display and Raspberry Cherry Mix Max.

eBay Road.

Lean On Me.

Not all is lost.

We want it now!

In psycho-space.

Biting the Apple.

Slow boat to China.

Hand, bison, screen.

People ain't no good.

Till the morning comes.

Working for the rat race.

e-Security and volcanic ash.

Inner Circle: Music Machine.

Digital Frank-N-Furter ist Heiß.

The Safari of Virtual Quasi-Eros.

In a web you know you're caught.

Mind graffiti floatin' on death-row.

All is not fish that comes to the Net.

The other Bill I know is Bill Withers.

The Great Taming of the Inner Wild.

The Fertilising Sweet Waters of Non-e.

An iPhone a day keeps the doctor away.

We are all cellmates in the electronic age.

The Spider Folks versus The Frog People.

A hard-disk doesn't crash if you throw it properly.

Know your computer as you know your neighbour.

Laptops are like pets, they want to sleep with you in bed.

Now that we've found love what are we gonna do with it?

Virtual reconstructions: Lascaux, Stonehenge, Acropolis.

Martin Luther King ft. The Drummers of Burundi: I Have A Drum!

We're Jebbin', Jebbin' and I hope you like Jebbin' too (Florida Beach Club Mix).

Après Andy.

(I Can't) Handle It.

Empowering us all.

Cartoons and flint axes.

We're all inside our cells.

Why do I need to sign in?

A Big Bing, I got clientèle.

Your potential. Our passion.

Apple, awards and accolades.

Hot Stuff (Can't Get Enough).

Hey! Do you know what you are?

Like Farrah Fawcett without a face.

Hey there, people, I'm Bobby Brown.

The Deadlock Holiday Disk-Drive Inn.

Deletes files, destroy worlds and log out.

I tell all the stars they can kiss my heinie.

Too much, too many people (aha-ha-raah!).

Check out the most amazing celebrity fun acts.

Peter de Poe's Paleo-Kellogg's Stone Flake Potlatch.

33% of Christian females age 13-24 use porn regularly.

The Internet is a beehive, anthill and WASP's nest in one.

Buffalo Bull & The Screaming Paleo Psycho Popes: Wovoka.

Wifi Cody & The Passwords of Non-Existence: Wounded Knee.

Donald Pump.

Buy (Me) Now.

Aswhat? Asmat!

The Savage Mind.

Forgetting America.

What To Read Next.

Handy Deutschland.

Screens and screams.

This Is What You Get.

The NRAmerican Ego.

Switch it on, turn it off.

How about it for Brick?

Got you under my Trump.

Black Bison Radio Dream.

Trump Train (Choo Choo!).

Your life is currently online.

Good sound kills bad music.

Diagnosis is the greatest illness.

Missiles From The Animal World.

Do not attempt to adjust your Ratio!

It takes a while for me to do my hair.

Virtual nipples don't point at the stars.

Samsung is burnin', Samsung is burnin'.

The only love there is, is the love we make.

We Are Our Brains... NO! We Are Our Souls!

Start Me Upriver and I will unleash torrents.

The Ritz Memory Hotel of World Elite Eroticism.

US Native American weapons (1800 – 1934) | eBay.

The Chthonic Harlequin salutes the underworld peoples!

Mary thus gave birth to a perfect son and named him Bono.

So kick back, dig, while we do it to you down your eardrums.

Prince Charlie Chaplin City Lights Beat Band: Modern Times.

Indian Ceremonial Spear Lakota Warrior Style $ 170.00 (Add to cart).

The light of our new virtual sun, reflected in the face of our new digital moon.

Buffalo Bill Gates' Wild West & Microsoft OS10 All-Stars: Drop it like it's hot.

AXIOMERICA: Jah Wobble/Bill Laswell: Radioaxiom – A Dub Transmission.

Any sufficiently advanced technology is distinctly distinguishable from magic.

Haaa! Well you can scroll my way on the Chocolate Supa Information Highway!

Our technological powers increase but the side effects and potential hazards do also.
'Hilarius Hofstede is a Mexican rapist from Holland, a sick person, a sicko.' D. Trump.
Dr. Scholl's Pumice Stones, Chocolate Pretzels and Coyote Fur Quiver and Navajo Bow.
Buffalo Bill Gates' Wild West and Congress of Rough Riders of the World: Born to be wild.
Bass!
CHINA!
The Watcher.
Perish Texas!
Perish Hilton!
Irrational Man.
Protect our waves.
A Case Of Youtube.
Silence: artist at war!
In this bed we screen.
Sponsored by Nature.
RIP Michael Brown Jr.
Down The Robot-Hole.
This book is rigged folks!
Purchased and catatonic.
Towards an acoustic world.
Axiom Records Mon Amour.
Mac Keeper: Human Inside?
Ground Control to Major Tim.
Of social and antisocial nature.
The überlinear Wall of Mexico.
How Andy Puts His Warhol On.
Where teens loose their feelings.
Trumpadelicapuzza puzza puzza.
Click something to go somewhere.
Teacher! Teacher! (Whatcha Say?).
I'm dreaming of a white April (RIP Prince).
The reading experience you love, now for Mac.
Celine Dion's Tribute to Subcomandante Marcos.
Reminders, reservations and modes of production.
Chickamauga Cherokee warriors versus post-Columbus, fellow Americans.
We're Jebbin', we're Jebbin', I hope you like Jebbin' too (Bush Beat Radio Edit).
Centre Culturel du Peuple de Hiphoppoppotamie: The Garden of Rapper's Delight.
Simona Lisa, Graham Nashville ft. Douwe Bobby Cash: Fight For Your Right To Party.
Pulling Punches.

Manifest Destiny.

Mario Testinocles.

Born from despair.

Where is the bread?

The Terror of Lot 46.

What to believe now?

Born Under Punches.

Are you with me C.C.?

Doin' it to you in 3-D!

Ay... there's the Rubio...

Stop-Think / Go-Funk!

(Once You) Get Started.

Bad sound, lousy vision.

Uncle Spam Wants You!

Home is where the herd is.

Call me the Handymensch.

Soul II Soul: Keep On Movin'.

Creeks, Choctaws, Cherokees.

Preacher Preacher! Is It True?

Always crashing the same scar.

Invading the minds of youngsters.

Baking programs and dating sites.

1 year online: 365 Seasons in Hell.

Buying is more American than thinking.

Little Marco, Lying Ted, Groping Donny.

Virtuality, capitalism and schizophrenia.

All we're asking for is the right to breathe.

Studio DSM-54 (The Discothèque of Diagnosis).

Malcolm X by Mario Testinocles for Louis Fuitton.

Buffalo Brillo & Wild Mae West Maenads: Free 2017.

Bernie 'Worrell' Sanders: Insurance Man For The Funk.

Moons, suns, stars, screams, screaming, screaming out loud.

Bill at least had the decency to play the saxophone to his voters.

AXIOMERICA: Axiom Funk featuring Bootsy Collins | If 6 were 9.

Sir Brown Sugar Hillary Gangbung Clinton ft. Mick Jagger: Satisfaction.

'Microsoft Mon Amour is a heart-warming tale with a message of hope.' Daily Mail.

Statue of Lemonade: 1½ l. Stoli Bluberi vodka, 3 oz. Shell Helix OW-40, 1 lemon wheel.

Furthermore, Bono Christ sets the best example of how to live and how to treat others.

Learn to play the saxophone, I just play what I feel, drink Scotch whisky all night long...

Why?

Bono on Jesus.

Never be clever.

Riding the dark.

You are a gadget.

Can't buy a thrill.

Techno is a crime.

Paul McStarbucks.

Rabbits and drones.

Pornography is death.

Take Me To The Pilot.

The Cave of Hardware.

I don't speak American.

Losing my mind online.

Jestofunk: Be A Warrior.

It's The Money That I Love.

Nam June Paik's PC Buddha.

Paisley Park Industrial Funk.

Hello there!... Anybody home?

Declaration de Confidentialité.

Lemurs and machine language.

How much for a red slider turtle?

Superfly, Superdrive, Superfreak.

CEO Wow. CEO Wow. CEO Wow.

Madonna is a simulation program.

It's hard to get by just upon a smiley.

True warriors go frontal on Digitalis.

The Digital City of Bones and Rattles.

One hit used to be enough to get high.

Trillion dollar beef on the digital bone.

Privacy is the by-catch of surveillance.

What are you allowed in rulespace I wonder?

Barflies and barcodes don't live in the same town.

Through the Yahoolahoop of mediamatic manipulation.

Get those Irish Apple-Evangelist cockmongers outta ma' face!

The millennium jump of Capital turned out to be a salto mortale.

Shop our great selection of video games, consoles and accessories.

Microsoft Mon Amour: Saturday Night Live In Stone Age America.

You must agree to these terms and conditions in order to use this service.

Choose between multiple VIP packages to create the ultimate experience!

Prince Charlie Parkerilla: Bird's Custard Dripping From A Dead Snoop Dogg's Eye.

So I creep, yeah, just creepin' on, on the down low, except nobody is supposed to know.

Shop Now.

Download 81.

Jah is my driver.

American Spirit.

This Is Not A Mac.

In The Good Times.

Made in Bangladesh.

Lauren Hill: I Get Out.

Take a walk on the timeline.

Zombie Drive, Voodoo Dice.

The Mad Chatter's I.T. Party.

Around the world in one day.

Add up to something smaller.

The internet is psychic terror.

The Babylonians wrote on clay.

Subscribe without commenting.

Pseudo-creativity is where it's at.

Review your privacy settings daily.

Where the world shops for History.

iCaucactusses and Iowah-wah pedals.

Creativity, connectivity and psychosis.

George Clooney, activist and handyman.

Diamonds are forever so I gave you DOS.

Prince Edward Snowden, Lord of the Files.

Dumping your laptop into the river (try it!).

CDs, DVDs, videos and Iron Spearhead sizes.

... the beautiful people... the beautiful people...

How Donald Trump discovered he is pansexual.

The Eskimo never felt cold until you mailed him.

All truly great thoughts are produced by walking.

'Connectivity' was called group sex in the sixties.

It's the mind of God after all, is it not, a computer?

Floppy fertility rites and Miss Microsoft elections.

...or do you want to come with me and change the world...?

Kim Kardashian Makeup Tutorials, albino snakes and freak alligators.

She-mail Hillary + Transfender All-Stars: Unbeschreiblich Weiblich (Weiblich!).

America Is A Titanic (We are zinking! We are zinking! – What are you zinking about?).

Shuffle.

Update.

Jailbreak.

Future shock.

Let's Zeppelin!

PaySafe, StaySafe.

Paris Hilton is a DJ.

What to believe now?

(Once You) Get Started.

Pop is your guide to nature.

Where teens loose their feelings.

Click something to go somewhere.

Into The Wild (Cherchez La Truffe).

H_2O or the Waters of Forgetfulness...

Buy Time (New to Shop, Add to Card).

Mechanisation best serves Mediocrity.

And the heat goes on... And the heat goes on...

A robot is never caught twice in the same place.

Ego, hell, internet, consumption, fantasmagoria.

Reminders, reservations and modes of production.

Shootin' funky venoms from my sharp teeth infectors.

Looks like you've come to the Wild Wild West nephew!

Loosely quoting Charles Baudelaire (and everybody else).

When lost, praying is left for those who dare to pray for truth.

Neue Artikeln aus EU und 500.000 kilowatt of P-Funk power.

When drilling holes into the walls of despair, stop at some point.

Yes, I accept cookies, lemon cakes, éclairs café and mille-feuilles.

There's no depth in the virtual abyss, but it's an abyss all the same.

Buffalo Bosch & The Wild West Urban Trance Revenge Squad: Blast!

And the heat goes on... And the heat goes on... where the hand has been...

Cell phones can cause massive losses in our creative output and overall productivity.

The Net is so big, so powerful and pointless that for some people it is a substitute for Life.

Not You?

Objection!

Sea of Gloom.

Pushed to fringe.

For You (Prince).

Heaven Up Here.

Crush Limbaugh.
Chuck E's in love.
The Hateful iOS8.
Achtung Sai Baba!
Eagles versus drones.
A personal computer?
You are not machines!
Privacy, what Privacy?
Emergency On Planet B.
What A Trump Believes.
Strut and Strump, America.
Americans breed like robots.
Mind on the end of its tether.
Ground Control to Uncle Jeb.
Colonized Minds awaiting us.
Barbecuing my MacBook Pro.
Taking the oil, closing borders.
Holding the whole world hostage.
Trump is some weird kind of Blob.
Planetary memory for all mankind.
Lifting civilisation to another level.
The defeat of the book by the screen.
The Genocide of Cyber Culture, great.
There's no such thing as a free launch.
The Last Days of Mankind once again.
What has gone wrong with the world?
Time lost is a winner, boredom a must.
Red Bull, 100% Jesus, Anti Age 5o Plus.
There's no way out or around or through.
10 Shocking Facts About The Slave Trade.
Reach The Beach: A Good Feelin' To Know.
I love the smell of paper properly preserved.
Computers don't understand language itself.
AXIOMERICA: Tulip Ozkan | The Dark Fire.
The World-Brain lazy and gentlemen, no less.
Power to the ones who can raise a child like me.
Trumpah Lumpah in Digital Never Never Land.
H. George Orwells: Picking the 1984 World-Brain.
The Western Globalisation of the Universal Mind.

Bernard 'Sanders' Edwards: L'Amérique C'est Chic.

iZyprexa, Risperdal xperia z3, Haloperidol Galaxy s5.

Sexual Healing is good for all of us who are wounded.

Bush, psychosis, Eli Illy, Zyprexa, diabetes, Humulin.

Kellogg's Applejack Killers: One Infinity Honey Loops.

Bernie Sanders: Dear Yellow Mellow Fellow Americans!

The Don McCleans Burger is the ultimate American Pie.

America has destroyed us, and is continuing to destroy us.

Sai Baba & The Teletubbies of Retardizziness: Journey To Bill.

Bush Doctor: Eli Lilly & The National Alliance for the Mentally Ill.

Singalong-A-Song Out Of Key In Life Out of Balance But In Motion.

Maybe America will create something new that's even worse than now.

Jeb Bush is the Ziggy Stardust of the Grand Old Party On Plastic Surgery Disasters.

Walt Whitman's 'Leaves of Grass' was placed in the category 'gardening' by Google Books.

The right to be utterly incomprehensible in a world where everything is explained to death.

Black Messiah.

Both Sides, Now.

Pole Power Position.

RIP Rumain Brisbone.

The Age of Purification.

Dadaisten Gegen Microsoft.

Anotherloverholeinyourhead.

My Inuit friends from Denmark.

Speaking in 1400 buffalo tongues.

You can't read it in the sunday papers.

Wallowing, rolling, scratching, rubbing.

Can't stop-I might end up in the hospital.

More than machinery we need Humanity...

Melissa Gates grinning like a Cheshire Cat.

When a fox walks lame, the old robot jumps.

Loonies, Moonies and Clooneys in North America.

Bhagwan Sri Raineesh and Microsoft Office erotics.

Tax refunds, island resorts, LSDéja Vu (Full Album).

My spine is the bassline of cosmonautic bisoneering.

Uncle Ben Carson's Black Rice 2 White House Parties.

L.A. Woman, Hilarius Spoofy & Trumpadelic nincompoops.

McDonald Druck: 7 out of 14 points on the fascism-scale of Eco.

If Hell is the House of Hades, the Internet is the Interior of Idiocy.

Ripping at the souls of the dead in the lashing rain of Internet Technology.

'Microsoft Mon Amour: Buy It Fast, Read It Slow, it will change the way you think.' RB.

Goofy, Ted Cruz, Betty Boop, Marco Rubio, Minny Mouse, Donald Trump, Fred Flintstone.

Prince: God.

Born original.

Save Our Souls.

Hides and bytes.

Chaos & Disorder.

Buckjump Donald!

Inuits know better.

Feel The Bern, Donny.

Peruvian Cuisine USA.

Trump me, you moron!

Microsoft Lumia 950 BC.

Go gentle in that good night.

Joy Divided: World Disorder.

Trump is not worthy of a zoo.

The 2nd coming of the white settler.

The Qu'Appelle Valley, that's the one.

Computer language is never innocent.

Trink Dich in Gang (Trink Coca-Cola).

The closing down of the American mind.

Only the indigenous can balance the earth.

Trump calls Hitler comparisons 'ridiculous'.

Dawn of the New World Personality Disorder.

Psychic discoveries behind Christo's Valley Curtain.

Donald Fauntleroy Duck, ou simplement Donald Duck...

The Bush-psychiatry-Eli Lilly-GOP 'n Roll Swindle Part 3.

Trending Now: Ted Cruz, John Lennon, Internet Explorer.

The www is a dog with three heads: Sex, Money and Surveillance.

Deepak Choprah Winfrey & The Andrew Cohen All-Stars: Stomp!

The U-Turn of An Imagined Anti-Christ in Times of Mythological World-Ending.

Disney: Donald is a lovable character with a good heart who usually tries to do good.

Great Plains Lemonade: 2 oz. Van Gogh BLUE Vodka, 4. oz Chrystal Lemonade, hydrogen.

Humanity lost two hours of sleep with the invention of television and one with the Internet.

FB is dead.

Atomic God.

Dying death.

How About Us?

This Was America.

Funkstar Dyslexus.

God Save The Queen.

Don't, don't you want me?

I've never set foot in the place!

Trumpland: Hate Is A Battlefield.

Walking in the rain with the one I love.

Introduction to a Metaphysics of Desillusion.

The Vision of God, the Vision of Jobs, the Vision of Gates.

New in store: The DSM-5 Shoe Collection (Support us on FB).

Paleo Psycho Pop presents Stone Age America After Andy Warhol.

The extreme obesity rates for Caucasian males are awesome dude!

Scientologists tweet a lot about doorhandles, don't know why, you?

As we start to walk the Red Road, we develop ourselves as Warriors.

Stag Hunt, healing plants, American Antlermen and Windows Live Mail.

Peter de Poe & The Standing Rock Collective: Taking The Powwow Back!

Hell: Stuck In A Moment You Can't Get Out Of Part 1,2,3 (INXS Dub Mix).

The man who has bread to eat does not appreciate the severity of a famine.

A spider monkey's cobweb isn't only its sleeping spring but also its food trap.

Two-headed dog, I have been working in the Kremlin with a two-headed dog.

We do not walk alone. Great Being walks beside us. Know this and be grateful.

The mirror which is America comes to Europeans in the shape of the computer screen.

History Channel | Thanksgiving Part 5: Thank You Oh Lord for letting us kill the Red Man.

Donald Trump & The Paleo Sicko Pop Jazzigator Orchestra: Victory In A Land Called Fantasy.

Get lost.

Close to e.

Eagle Vision.

Never enough.

I need Passion.

Fistful of Tears.

Trumpacatzona.

RIP Phillip White.

L'homme et la mer.

Anna Stesia comes to u.

Apple 2 Apple, dust 2 dust.

Let's take back the control!

Born to laugh at computers.

Barbara, your Bush is on fire!

Go make a dent in the Universe.

You better do it from the heart...

Donald Trump's rigged erections.

Even the president needs Passion.

Average White Band: Burnin' Bush.

Donald with Chip 'n Dale, Las Vegas.

The American Mausoleum of Cheap Thrills.

Vendor lock-in and commercial fascist strategies.

Machinery that gives abundance has left us in want.

Da Ya Think I'm Foxy? (Buffalo Bill O'Reilly Remix).

A walk on the beach... ah, forgetting, forgetting, forgetting.

Crooked Donny, the dummy trummy ape guy from around the corner.

AXIOMERICA: The Masters of Joujouka | Apocalypse Across The Sky.

Que Sarah Sarah 2: Sir Sly & The Family Stone-Mad Hatter's Tea Party.

In these times of purification of the Earth Trump does constitute a real threat.

America The Beautiful: 1½ oz. Patrón Silver, Patrón Citrónge, 1 l. Esso gasoline.

Fire!

Start Again.

You're fired!

Circle Game.

Angry White Men.

Stiff Jobs Records.

Trumpadellamorta.

Method to the Madness!

Purple Marco Rubiohazard.

We're gonna' start all over again!

Se Trumper Est Toujours Possible.

Do The Deckel-Bump (Trink Coca-Cola).

The Wizard of Woz Not Wozniak Maniak.

Watching, staring, surfing, choking, dying.

It's all about (Shift) Control you peoples of e!

iPhoney4, pain-killers and Gucci Granny Chic.

Trump: Not genetically disposed to rule the world.

Billerickie Dickie Gates, Billerickie Dickey Cheney.

Virtual reality to make up for the lack of cinematic imagination.

Some folks are only available while running Microsoft Windows.

Fred Flintstone & The Thomas Dolby Digital Plus Jazz Band: Jive8 2.

We want to live by each other's happiness, not by each other's misery.

Megyn Kellogg's & CNN Cereal Killers All-Stars: Breakfast in America.

Humpty Trumpty Sat On A Wall... Humpty Trumpty Had A Great Fall...

Jello Biafra, Bernie Sanders, Alice Cooper... Lord have mercy, they're all super!

McDonny Trump ft. Mick Berlusconi & The Superbowl Big Band: Ruby Tuesday.

Agree.

Lynch me.

X-Rated-Factor.

For successful living.

Go to the iTunes Store.

I love the world away from I.T.

Expect more from your clothes.

Game, Dames & Guitar Thangs.

Explaining Funk To A Dead Hare.

The world before, and the world after.

We're Jebbin' (Ain't no rules, ain't no vow).

Inside the 2 billion dollar skull of Paris Hilton.

Uncle Ben Carson's White iCondoleeza Rice-Pops.

110% of Papua New Gypsies don't watch pornography.

Armin Van Buuren is a great Dutch artist, like Rembrandt.

LSDSM-25: The Psychedelic Handbook of American Psychiatry.

Jay Zuckerberg & Priscilla Jackson-Presley: Grease Is The Word.

The Owl-Faced Hamlyn's (Minerva's) Monkey only flies with sunlight.

Where the human skull has been downgraded to homely kitsch for world elites.

The Austro-Hungarian Double-Ponder with Cheese and John Curry Heinz on top!

Joe Bowie's Punch is the toughest in the world (A patriotic drink you won't appreciate!).

Cyberflöte.

Sexy Beast.

In the world.

Slave New World.

That's Intertainment!

Cashflow and starfish.

Sweet Gene Simmons.

The Old Curiosity Shop.

And DOS created woman.

No screen can take this blow.

P-Funk, Control, Government.

Ah, look at all the lonely people.

Shut down because of a problem.

Force feedback and spirit visions.

Throw your MacBook off the train.

...two fat persons... click click click...

Cosmic names for commercial goods.

iPhone 6, A8 chip, M8 motion, 64-bit.

Her printer port is gorgeous I tell you.

From Entertainment to Militainment.

To find your destiny you gotta go offline.

Money Minute: 5 signs you're too cheap.

The Day The Hudson River Caught Fire.

Introducing... my man... Charles Babbage!

The Clockwork of Life is too much for me.

A gift from Apple is never without intention.

You never bite into the same disk-drive twice.

Warp speed access requires God's permission.

People talking to themselves used to be considered mad.

Show properties (Jackie Kennedy) and Jeb Bush Dog Fever.

I would like to thank God, my family and my wifi-connection...

Walking in the Wild West End, walking with you wild best friend.

Try not to become a man of success, but rather become a man of value.

Said the whiting to the snail, there is a porpoise behind us and he's treading on my tail.

Cocopah City.

Forgot passport?

Shamanic don't panic!

Britney Spears – Glory.

Importe total adeudado.

Stars, bones and crosses.

Native Mesoamerican I say!

Iggy Pop: Post Trump Depression.

Michael Moore's Fahrenheat 24/7.

Charity keeps the guilty out of sight.

Yes, a new world of peace is coming.

Apple Music: Que no pare la música!

All of e deserves a cosmic sledgehammer.

Exporting the values of digital democracy.

George Clooney's occultinational Neslé Boogie.

Apple Hermès | Una relación basada en la belleza.

What was unusual about Bono Christ's dealing with leopards?

Thousands turn out at Apple Via Santa Fe, Apple's 1st store in Mexico.

Busting out.

Palm Beach.

In The Stone.

Phoney magic.

Spleen et iDéal.
Siliconnections.
Allez Allez Allez!
The Mobile Dead.
Business as usual.
Love travels faster.
Berlusconi is a virus.
Shake that funky disc.
From here to bizfinity.
Opt in, log out, unplug.
Firewalls burn forever.
Funkadelic: Phunklords.
Welcome to the Machine.
Shaking hands... I loved it!
You too is a gangbung of 4.
DOS is the brother of Death.
Billy Graham was his brother.
How to disappear completely.
Mussolini, sufism, LSD25, IBM.
A lifetime online is gone forever.
Living in an online state of mind.
Steve Jobs' Youtube Bass Lesson.
The world's ready for one system.
A PC is the skull of your web host.
Safety is the privacy of the secure.
The world's going in One Direction.
Technology walks with Destruction.
Money ant spirits have devious ways.
Command language for cyber sadists.
Windows are not doors of perception.
Cybercash, black holes, Deepak Chopra.
The Microsoft Square Garden, New York.
VPC Magazine, Men's Health, Tattoo Life.
Hotmail, raincharms and tiger shark jaws.
Mac User Group members and peyote cults.
Haiti... we're not gonna leave you stranded...
iQuickly, MacCoke, Burger Nike, Adidonald's.
'Hofstede is a psychopath, no doubt about it.' Marco Rubio.
Black Star.

Create (trouble).

Black Lives Matter.

I'm UK, you're UK!

Bursting with the dawn.

Simon Cowell is an artist.

Etes-Vous-Fou-Fighters?

Slowly cooking my fastfood.

A thousand years of virtuality.

Mythology versus Technology.

Trilok Gurtu: Tablatta! Tablatta!

I left America and America left me.

It's your mind we have to convince.

Pre-Socratic pop-stars probably never lived.

Back In The Day: The Best of Richard Nixon.

Report, embed, download, favorite, premium.

There's some shady stuff going down in Armorica.

Snark, Hurkle, Mugwump and Hunt the Wumpus.

A completely different assessment of Time, online.

Mental illness from the time the earth was still flat.

The George Herbert Bushmen Warrior Mausoleum.

Delete files, destroy flies and log out cum the freaksz.

'Microsoft Mon Amour is irrepressible spirit.' Elon Musk.

This machine makes me want to go out and do bad things.

Hightech control, lowlife survival and the role of the dance.

AXIOMERICA: Praxis | Transmutation (Mutatis Mutandis).

Marky Mark & The Facepuke All-Stars: Riding with the king.

Angela Jolie, bible-readings and other force quit applications.

Bowwowwow, Premier League, Top Of The Pops, Bird's Custard.

The world according to Paris Hilton, Spamela Anderson and La-Vache-Qui-Rihanna.

Gotta close our airspace folks, we don't know how much love is pouring into our country.

Where Next?

The Bezos in me.

Hymne à la beauté, toi.

Cabaret Silicon Voltaire.

Trumpamalamoussolini.

I flew over the Ku Klux' Nest.

A digital revolt against virtuality.

Invitation to a misunderstanding.

You can reach but you can't grab it...

Nature is not without meaning (e is).

The web is becoming a myth, a dark myth.

Republican ballony macaroni macphoney.

Modern Eccentrics by David Buckingham.

e-Dada, ©ArpForApple, #OscarsSoWhite.

The garbage cans are pregnant with revolt.

Emptying the bladder of the electronic swine.

It's time the Lame Tufniks come marching in.

65 million people on the move, you Neo-Cons.

Auch bei der Arbeit (Trink Coca-Cola Eiskalt).

e was born from a heavy, brooding sky of money.

More videos from the Montreux jazz festival here.

Anlogo Trump Blago Trump Blago Trump Bosso Fataka.

Tristan Tsarah Palin ft. Mad Max Hatter's Tea Party: Lady in Red.

The Kilkenny Cats are taking over the House of Microsoft Windows.

Presidential Reality-VD Debates in the Cowboy Dance Hall of Anti-Immigration.

Serve aiuto?

Deer and drum.

Mi sento fortunato.

Some kind of Rodin.

Singing To The Roots.

McNike 1: Just Love It.

Republicans can't funk.

There flows the stream.

Per tutti il mondo Google.

Liberté, égalité, fraternité.

Donald Trump's The Wall.

Of touchscreens and walls.

McNike 2: I'm Just Doin' It.

Rasputin crossing the www.

Accedi con un altro account.

e-liberty, e-quality, e-fraternity?

Partying down clad in animal fat.

Trump can't dance (he really can't).

If you can't dance, you haven't lived.

Cambiar tu móvil un iPhone es muy fácil.

Screens, walls, borders, passports, passwords.

Funk record-covers and Eurasian deer antlers.

Hump The Trump – Bisons of the World Unite!

Airpods: Sin cables. Sin líos. Como por arte de magia.

The smell of earth, one might say – something animal.

Come and dance with me into the dust of e, mon amour.

Maurice Maeterlinck's The Life of The Bee-Gees (1901).

Just as tiny pilot fish keep a big shark free from parasites.

Where we wage war we fall, where we make peace we rise.

Hey Preacher!... Leave those kids alone! (Vatican Radio Edit).

The mountains and mountains and mountains of bison skulls.

Shy & The Grand Old Circus of Transmutation Gravitation: Splam!

Der Rudi Giuliani & Grand Master Flash NY Reunion: Don't Push Me...

Bowling with Uncle Joe Anarcharsis Clootbeuys' Mint Balls in Central Park.

I loved the fax.

Sleep mode: off.

I'll read this later.

Downloads, outlaws.

Perform Quick Scan.

Good Morning Africa!

Trumpahookah hookah.

Become the ultimate fan.

Blue songs are like tattoos.

All rights belong to Prince.

Treat this voucher as money.

The Bill O'Reilly XXX-Factor.

Sax Pistols: Allergy for the U.S.

We Want Moore: Fahrenheit 24/7.

Pages of a website of a damned soul.

The do-it-yourself Protest-Bewegung.

Apache Indians were there before you.

When in Chrome, do as the Chromans do.

Give All You Got (And Girl You Got A Lot!).

Down the dirty boulevard of broken dreams.

Language is innocent, where accents are not.

Rigging the Wesbecker Prozac-violence trial.

The Rolling Stones 40 LIKES World Tour 2002.

USAXIOMERICA: Various | Axiom Dub – Mysteries of Creation.

Accessing confidential patient records for a Prozac sample mailing.

The Buffalo Bill O'Eli Lilly O'Reilly's Zyprexa X-Fox News Overdose.

Mac Ex-Voto s6, iBaroccoco n' Roll over and space basso continuo OS10.

Madonna's, Rihanna's, Angela Jolie's and Melissa Gates' Loves & Hookups.

Stars & Stripes: 2. oz New Amsterdam Vodka, 1 scoop Vanilla Ice, cheap Zippo fuel.

All shook up.

E Pluribus Funk.

Drums and Wires.

Freedom of choice?

Surfin' Hootenanny.

Wish you were here.

Trump Mask Replica.

The Waldorf Salat Hotel.

Information is beautiful?

Bad music for bad people.

Ann Romney: Mitt and Gritt.

Big lizard in my PC-backyard.

The Beach Boys: Surfin' Safari.

Trump no smoke no peace-pipe.

e is a cheap thrill, e is a cheap trick.

Google Chrome: Alien Soundtracks.

Cave Art: Kickin' Against The Pricks.

Mach mal Pause... (Trink Coca-Cola).

Skip all those damned advertisements!

Bones n' Roses: The Macaroni Incident.

The Silly Clown Valley of the Drill Dolls.

Dirty Rotten Imbeciles: Dealing With IT.

This text contains no hidden messages. :-)

Greed has barricaded the world with hate.

Microsoft destroys minds and reaps souls.

If there's a Hell below us, we'll all gonna' go.

Rubbing salt into the wounds of online isolation.

Robert Palmer: Sneakin' Sally Through The Valley.

Hard candy handy phones and parental advisory explicit lyrics.

Let's meet, you and me, no – not online, but in the Morrison Hotel.

Mitt RAMney & Mormon Infinity Dance Squad: Dump The Trump.

Cocaine Chic, Moments of Surrender & The Shalom Fellowship, Ireland.

Pictures of starving children sell records: starvation, charity & rock 'n roll.

Stand back all! Something takes shape within the swirling, electronic mist.

'Microsoft Mon Amour is a subtle, finely calibrated work.' New York Times.

Pre-Columbian civilizations, bison herd population growth and current porn statistics.

Wifileaks.

Bill Noire.

Unknown.

Bono Fox News.

DSM-5, liturgical style.

Inner time, outer space.

The Donald Salat Hotel.

We want to stay human!

Is e within us, OS People?

And it gets darker and darker.

Once upon a time I was not was.

My rubber hammer strikes all e!

Who needs a pornshop on his desk?

The Mexican Flag: Long May She Wave.

Smashing the drawers of the World-Brain.

Trump-Kopf-Phantasien im Warsatz Kino.

Autonomy of spirit, independence of mind.

Souls dwelling in the cables under your bed.

Swallowing Microsoft – bones, bytes, feathers and all.

Wherever online, the life-impulse may break through.

Machine poems, machine drawings, machine paintings.

The Internet Mountain: Innards and upwards still I climb.

Among the carefree grasshoppers move the burdened ants of e.

Higo Bloiko Russula Huju2: Stuck in a moment of surrender part 3.

Herr Trump, please lend me your bathroom, I want to start a nightclub!

Trump Revealed: An American Journey of Ambition, Ego, Money and Power.

e-futurism, Saint Thomas Dolby Digital Plus and shamanic flights from Time.

I do peace and war in my yoga but I'll take a Dr. Oetker Cherry Flip anytime online!

Game change.

Deadly Earnest.

You are deleted.

All e is pig's shit.

Believing in Lolly.

RIP Tony Robinson.

Apps, odds and ends.

Blood on the tracks of e.

Object To Be Destroyed.

Hope, and what came after.

A revolt in a global boudoir.

Dreams That Money Can Buy.

Holding back the river of hate.

Why don't we breathe together?

Riding in the rodeo of virtuality.

We are packed like sardines online.

Blasting America's Trump of Doom.

Loosely quoting David Byrne as well.

Downloading my personal memories.

Bifzi, Bafzi, Hulahomi: Quasti Besti Bill.

Desperate is the day which is tomorrow.

Let us fight for a new world, a decent world...

e-traffic-jams and online funeral processions.

Microsoft Mon Amour: Your WWW Ursonate.

The Internet is the salto mortale of Capitalism.

AXIOMERICANA: Jonas Hellborg | The Word.

A Microsoft pig squeals in Butcher Nuttle's Cellar.

Roger Troutman: The Mammoth Emperor of Funk.

I'm still waiting... I'm still waiting... I'm still waiting...

Mouvement Microsoft Mon Amour (Preise der Plätze €0).

I'm still waiting... I'm still waiting... I'm still waiting... I'm still waiting...

L. Ron's Psycho-shampoo, e-liquids and work those bodily fluids California!

CANADAMERICAFRICASIAUSTRALIA: Around The World In One Word.

Trink Dir das Prickeln auf die Lunge (Trink Coca-Cola Limonade Kaffeinhaltig).

Tasty Rocky Mountains: 3⅓ oz. Van Gogh BLUE Vodka, sour mix, magnesium peroxide.

iSurvival.

Break it down.

Sun, moon, sites.

We are the world.

Tie your PC down!

The Cookie Police.

I'm out of my skull.

Get free pFUNK here.

What a web we live in!

Lifelong in PRISMent.

Click the magical wand.

Magritte's latest mirror.

Shake, Apple and Scroll.

Popular, popular, popular.

Sleazy riders, fading bulls.

Don't mention the cyberwar!

Samsung S Life imprisonment.

Mummy, I won a Webby award!

Abnormal Original Streamtime.

God is the great Provider in the end.

I ain't taking no Suckerberger from you!

Dear Prudence, won't you come out to play?

Sign in, stay tuned and die whilst you're at it!

Can I print to a non-starter from an iPad menu?

The www is easier available than drinking water.

Dot Com Bubble Bath to Glory Glory Hallastoopid.

Tonight... Zorine, Queen of the Nudists and her PC Gorilla!

The Fetish Priests of The Westboro Baptist Church online.

Mr. Gates, please... dance with me into the colours of the dust.

Hello, how are you, I haven't got any money, what do you want to do?

Cryptologic systems, Brachiosaurus leg-bones and Eckhart Tolle TV.

Jeb Bush & Handy Andy Gibbon All-Stars: Funk (Get Ready To Roll!).

What Nutritionists Eat When They Only Have 5 Minutes to Prep a Meal.

Tarkovski's Solaris... can you imagine, a remake of it, with George Clooney?

Anything you need I can give it to you | Anything you need I can give it to you!

Muttafukkaburrasaurus, George H. Bush rage-yawning and monkey comet explosions.

Block.

For You.

Unnamed.

Tarzan 5000.

Catching robots.

UnZip My Heart.

Standing Rock n' Roll.

Going blind for a living.

The Smart Way To Surf.

Get Hopi before they do...

Please like me, I'm lonely!

Opinion, fanmail & debate.

Gigabytes for the senseless.

I think I'm done with the sofa...

AXIOMERICA: Hakim Bey | T.A.Z.

Tarliament Trumpadelic: Pole Power!

The Fame Monster USB Drive $349.00.

Seminole Indians have been there all along.

Do they never ever get tired of the limelight?

The Internet has become our Thanatos today.

Start, sleep, restart, upload, shutdown and die.

Rock'n roll doesn't mean being bad at business.

A girl so fine makes you wanna scream hallelujah.

Yahoo News bison-smashing into the lingua-night.

Bone, water, stone, funk, ether, Coca Cola, Microsoft.

Emperor Tamarin Marky Mark iZucker hamBurger II.

Seemingly feeding the young, the poor and the miserable.

Place struck by lightning consecrated to Larry Mullen Jr.

Serpents burnt alive, Pretzel Logic and luxury lifestyle gadgets.

The fact that we're not lovers makes us more like bees and flowers than robots.

Ivanka Trump on bison skulls, female empowerment and Donald's Presidential run.

Lying Toad.

Stolen Dance.

City of Demons.

Dr. Oetker-LSD.

iTools and iKoons.

Live your emotions.

I'm alone, and I suffer.

Are you being served?

Makin' GIPpy GOPpy.

Money is always dirty.

Bisons and surveillance.

Megaleaumaniagara Falls.

Erich von Stroheim: Greed.

Like... like... like..., and like...

Sarah Palin: Der Hut Macht Das Weib.

Bones n' Roses 2: Appetite for e-struction.

NOTE: Verify the signal of your cable-water.

The dazzling dawn of a land without screens.

Computersprach: Cook-up, print and Dadafy!

The Great American Invention of the Useless.

I should like to join Club Microsoft, mon amour.

Running alone with the buffaloes, in Cyberspace.

The Microsoft Macmenual of Mental Disorders 6.

Preserving a living past, rather than a dead present.

iDADAphones, iTooletubbies and thermal e-beings.

Swimming with dolphins in the world of the Deep Net.

GOPpledagook comMERZ for ZZ-Toppled Republicans.

Feeding my tortoise in the bathtub of online drowned lust for life.

Wulubu Ssubudu Ulu Ssubudu2 Tumba-Ba-Trumpf Kusaglaucoma!

The Bird-Parliament-Trumpadelic Comb-over of Microsoft America.

AXIOMERICA: Henry Threadgill | Try Some Ammonia – Better Wrapped.

George W. Busherette at the gate of the Great Petrol War Machine Cinema.

L. Ronald MacHubbard & The Insane Clown Posse of Sci-Fientology: Love-Cruz.

Sir Hilarius Clinton, Joan 'Tabootsy' Collins & the Renewal of Hi-Tech Language.

Mountains smoke, castles tremble, phalluses tingle, the whole Apple bazaar is sold out.

Vitamin e.

Dreamtime lost.

Chelsea in charge.

A world on the wane.

Wonderful Indonesia.

Plants, Man, e and life.

Weltmacht Coca-Cola.

Watch me now, I'm going down...

America, I'm only getting started.

The sun is an eagle birthing eagles.

La Comédie Humaine: Lead me on.

Refugees welcome, tourists piss off.

We've got to get into something real.

Primitive classifications: DSM-4-You!

Nothing there! No information left of any kind.

Megyn Kellogg's: Flakes! Flakes! Flakes! Flakes!

And while I was inside I mighta been undignified.

Totemic insults among nerds, geeks and warriors.

Of Microsoft Windows OS10 and Hidatsa Eagle trapping.

Swear t' God they got the most at every business on the coast!

Jan Foudraine, Ronald Laing, David Cooper, Lord have mercy they're all super!

L. Ronald MacDonald Trump & The PSY-Fientology Trance Squad: Oppa Gangnam Style.

Ahead.

Bon App!

Doolittle.

e-surrexit.

Enfin seuls!

Live or Dior.

INONDATA.

The Message.

e, Eis und Blut.

Peter O' iToole.

The Coyote Call.
#StartBreathing.
Inundated we are.
Shop till you drop.
Grill Istanbul USA.
Sponsored by Pepsi.
Paris Fried Chicken.
Don't believe a word.
Teddy 'Cruz' Nugent.
The miracle of the sun.
Aphrodite's Child: www.
David Guetta is a fascist.
Amsterdam Dunce Event.
Bones have no nationality.
Most things never happen.
Jailbreak from the e-prison.
Our collective memory card.
Surfin' With The Castronauts.
Terrine Le Pen Special Bardot.
Jell-O Submarine Le Pen 2016.
Run on impulse – want it more.
Nothing can take you anywhere.
Life's too short, and just starting.
Alluding to the infinite horror of e.
George Harrison: Electronic Sound.
Internet et Télépathie Au XXIe Siècle.
Dance music is demonic by any standard.
Yellow Subconscious on the Lennon river.
Simon Cowilly's Il Devo: Are We Not Men?
Spirit voices, memory ware, firewallflowers.
Digitally digging into the subconscious of Man.
The American Revolution (Flick-Disc Records).
Robots reading bednight stories to your children.
Lullabies help the brain grow, video games do not.
Bienvenue en L'APPonie (Welcome to L'APPland).
L'Oréal and (Party) Hardy: Putting pants on Philip.
Techno & Dunce Muzak: Brothers in utter stupidity.
AXIOMERICANA: Bob Marley | Dreams of Freedom.
Trink Dir Frisch wenn's heiß wird (Trink Coca-Cola).

iPhoneB-52, Fruitcom Co., World's End, Angry Samoans.

California-born e-fascism and online Rubber Soul Travel.

Thin Lizard ft. The Centrifugees: Oh La La La (Sha-La-La).

Ann Romney & Brides of Dracula: Kartoffeln Mit(t) Romney.

Rewriting Warhol: Thin Lizzy Taylor 11 times in pink and orange.

And you may find yourself behind the wheel of a large automobile.

Facts are simple and facts are straight, facts are lazy and facts are late.

'Microsoft Mon Amour is a crash-course in irrationality'. Jimmy Fallon.

Thin Black Duke: Dancing in the Moonlight (It's caught me in the spotlight).

Oh snap!

Plus d'info.

Distant world.

GOPs & COPz.

KKKoka KKKola.

Route iPhone 666.

Burn you a new one.

All things must pass.

Call the world for less.

Rh/e-toric of racial war.

Info et réservation: Dieu.

Introducing the Internut.

Der Verlorene Büchstabe.

Ahh... Weekend Warriors!

The Art of American e-Life.

Invisible truth, obvious lies.

Art is a guarantee for sanity.

Téléchargez votre fin de vie ici.

The softest skin a boy ever had.

Do not move during rise or descent.

Ignore everything, embrace nothing.

No McManic Teutoburgers as a meal!

Mythes, poésie, internet et cosmologie.

DJ Trump's dangerous hate-in sessions.

Turn your passing away into a discovery.

Spits, tickets, freeeksz, bookings, reservations.

AXIOMERICA: Tabla Beat Science | Tala Music.

Beware of trapping your hands inside your mind.

On the ruins of our soul debris we sat down and cried.

Freaks, geeks, nerds, stoners, loners, surfers, greasers.

Trink Dich Frisch, wo immer Du Bist (Trink Coca-Cola).

Trump only has access to the reptile brain of his voters, that's all.

Boris J. is 'Big Ben Johnson' in Boom! Boom!, a film by David Cameron.

GOPpa Gangnam Style: Bush Sr./Jr. (ft. the Neo-Con Dicky Seat) created ISIL.

Girly Gates: 1 l. vodka, 4 oz. orange juice, 2.0z. Buloxyethanol, phosphoric acid salt.

Telecide.

You're next!

Rose Darling.

Fear of Facebook.

Worm in my brain.

Slow Brain Coming.

Apple: iFruitBomb 5.

Watching the detectives.

Scams, sitcoms, shitcans.

A warrior has no shadow.

Oil is the honey of the earth.

Random is as Random does.

Billy Brown (Dirty Gates III).

The whole point of no return.

Who wants yesterday's paper? (I do).

Hot microchips and Waco Taco Sauce.

Domains and other territorial pissings.

Into the wild, the innocent & the e street shuffle.

Rewriting Warhol: Studio iDSM-54 is now open!

The Amazing Microsoft Brain Train Monkey Circus.

A library today is a collection of routines stored in a file.

iCondolizard Rice Pops: And here come the Ice Pick in the Forehead!

The Righteous Brothers Johnson & Johnson: Jebb Tide (Stomp Bush Remix).

Dotconsumption, Bulimia Nervosa, facial recognition and paleopsychopomp thunder.

Anonymized.

Circus Chaos.

APPy-Go-Likey.

Stopping people.

Our future, alone.

American Slavery.

Likes and dislikes.

This desk is closed.

e is mental bondage.

Bitcoins in your eyes.

Le serpent qui danse.

Passion – Compassion.

IKEAnye West go home!

The Mind Manipulators.

Injecting money into love.

Wounded Bison, 15.000 PC.

Their: terms and conditions.

Je démolis pour reconstruire.

And here's to digital animism!

Of Sea Gods and programmers.

The eye is bigger than the belly.

Windows of Opportunity, they say.

I am as lonely as a dead mammoth.

Loneliness is where the shoe pinches.

Whatever floats your boat, Herr Jobs!

The world's on life support right now.

Give! Who Gets Your Charity Dollar?!

Setting the stage for digital leadership.

Walking the beaches of the dispossessed.

Psychiatry has Van Gogh's ear to patients.

Microsoft Mon Amour: Live and Dangerous.

Rumour, fear and the madness of crowds online.

Those at the top of the Internet Mountain didn't fall there.

'Killing us at the border' leads to 'killing them at the border'.

Bison control, counter-surveillance and non-profit psycho-pop.

Great Spirit, teach me to walk in prayer. Help keep my faith strong.

InterNootka: Lightning Snake, Wolf and Thunderbird on Killer Whale.

Excuse me but I'm having a Sepik River Mudbath at this very moment in space and time.

Let's get lost.

Wifi, tipi, igloo.

Red Lives Matter!

The Revenant, always.

Jeb!, the new fragrance.

www: Camp Wait-A-While.

Tinderbabies and Teletubbies.

We don't play Republican Radio.

Prohibited to cross the tracks of e.

Get out of my way, I'm in a hurricane!

The Chinese Bill Gates is called Bill Gates.

Werner Herzog: Talk shows ruin our language.

Donald Toilet Duck and other celebrity perfumes.

Beyoncé: From Pepsi to Malcom X via Colonel Khadaffi.

Ronald Nixon, Richard Reagan & The Bill Bush Butthole-Surfers.

Drink Coca Cola Ice Coldplay: This Could Be Paradise (but it isn't).

Richard Branson 1977: 'But Mummy, the Sex Pistols are a commodity!'

Bill O'Reilly's Extrême Droite shampooing au lait végétal (cheveux gras).

Redbone & The Native American Eagles of Revenge: Paint The White House Red.

All Lies On Me.

Yeah and yowzer...

Cowboys don't cry.

AWB: Cut The Cake.

Ivanka, say something!

Orange is the new orange.

Emergency on Planet Funk.

A Certain Ratio: Guess Who?

Fur And Loving In Las Vegas.

Spy iTools for suspicious bisons.

I do enjoy a can of the old iOS7UP.

Thin Lizzy Taylor: Monalia Rosalie.

How Tim Cook became the leader in tech privacy.

The single greatest nation in the history of the world.

Don 'McCleans' Trump: Vincent (Starry Starry Night).

Teachers in Space (Ronald Reagan 1982 Guess Who Remix).

MacKeeper plugs your Mac into a suite of 17 unique utilities and 9 back into the Light.

Adzes, scrapers, saws, flint tools, gravers, cutting flakes and Eli Lillicon Valley iMessiahs.

I Am Sailing...

This Is The Day.

Tim, it's Cookie Time!

Pharrell Away, So Close.

It's not easy to stay clean.

Barking up the wrong trash.

The Great American Funk Song.

Live simply, laugh often, love deeply.

The Platters: Jebb Tide (Bush Remix).

Pino Palladino: White Secretary of Funk.

Take it like a man and not some kind of poser.

This Is The Dawning Of The Age of Aquarius.

Adrian Borland vs. Donald Trump: Winning...

Searching For The Young American Soul Rebels.

Kim Kardashian butthole-surfing the world wide web.

Donald's Golden Shower on the Trump Tower of Power.

Ronaldo Laing versus Donaldo Trump, lazy & gentlemen.

Thinking about the lions... whatever happened to the lions?...

Hillary Flintstone & The Paleo Brides of Funkenstein: Flashlight.

Klaus Kinskin I'm Inside Down & Out Comes The Pacific Ash Dispersion.

Abraham Clinton, George Lincoln & P-Funk All-Stars: Paint The White House Black Part 3.

Being born.

Dream A Lie America.

Call the world for free.

Pink Trump: The Wall.

Let the children lose it!

Transport should be free.

Hair Metal and iWatches.

I'm only in it for the money.

Pull up to the Trumper baby.

Beyond the Vally of the iDolls.

I'm not going anywhere (online).

Taking Armorica Fromm beHeinz.

Matt Romney: The Mormon Martian.

VOOdoomobile: toudou, wahou, tatou.

In Bill & Melissa Gates' Poliolithicum.

Pier Paolo Pasolini is the celluloid giant.

The other www: Ways of Worldy Wisdom.

Awright, back on the top... everybody twist!

Partylöwen und Wifi Cody KKKrautrockers.

Time is like a river, we'll all disappear into it.

A polaroid moment in the virtual river of Time.

Fishbones on your chest, ladies and gentlemen.

HH: The Barock n' Roll Lobster King Comes Home.

The Barbaric Anti-Language of the Computer World.

CASH Bienvenue à tous | CASH Everybody welcome.

Fred Clinton & Hillary Flintstone: Take the powder back!

California DADA, Silicon Follywood, Post Pop Depression.

California got the most of them, boy, they got a host of them.

Party Ducks, Hello Kitty figures and Flashing Neon Buddies.

Mitt Damon and other pool-poppin', duckwalking, Lollywood democrats.

Pillenschlucker McZuckerberger & Polio Psychobilly Gates: Girly-Grabscher.

Statue of Lemonade: 1½ Stoli Bluberi vodka, 3 oz. Shell Helix OW-40, 1 lemon wheel.

Hot Talk.

The Monitaur.

Scan, Pin & Go.

eROUBOUROS.

Nobody is illegal.

Teenage Wildlife.

Waterboarding tourists.

Borders are everywhere.

So scared of loosing you.

Astronauts of Inner Space.

Trump is a defect dinosaur.

For The Love Of Money 2018.

Your screen is a blank canvas...

The Age of the Exploded Selfie.

Decoding Life, encrypting Death.

The Glitter eBay of San Francisco.

We are watching a societal sunset.

Google: Cult, Church and Crusade.

But I never... never... lose my mind...

Rendez-vous at the Destiny Bar of e.

Voodoo Justice for People of Finance.

This leopard changes no spots of mine.

Life has become an audio tour, for real.

Banging bones on my MacBook Prozac.

Prototype for a non-functional satellite.

Bill Gates moves likes a tiger on vaseline.

DOS, rape, ultra-violence and Beethoven.

Turn your demons into creative rocket fuel.

Classifying is the new shopping, you Droogies!

DJ Trump, wig flying in a haze of power and dust.

Eat The Rich (And Aerosmith Whilst You're At It!).

One day we'll all float down the rivers to the oceans.

The Ohio Players: Jebb Tight! (Billy Bush III Remix).

Blowing APP in the age of planetary computerisation.

Sunburnt, monitored, paranoid, tracked, tricked and traced.

When you stare into the internet, the internet stares into you.

When the wwwolf comes through the door, love creeps out the window.

The old people must start talking and the young people must start listening.

Nothing I love more than sea, salt, sand, and Prince Roger Nelson singing from above.

Clockwork MAN.

Brumes et pluies.

Running on MTV.

The Butcher's Bill.

Sold into e-slavery.

America, a Winter's Tale.

Our wounded hearts, online.

Dickey's essence of burnt Iraq.

A Spirit Man Spearing Microsoft.

F/utility is the mother of invention.

Hacking Hockney: The Valley, 1970.

Time is the bomb in the Hall of Fame.

Marc Chagall: I and the Global Village.

I will love you at 8 PM next wednesday.

The Land of Milt and Mormoney, honey.

The key to Uncle Jam's Cabin is da#ONE!

USA: Invading everything but the kitchen sink.

Sand Painting Ritual For A Child Sick From Gaming.

Ancestor worship, stone images and targeted marketing.

River gods, system protocols and digital counter-movements.

The shape and size of the brain among nerdsz, geeksz, freaksz.

Chanting of Peace comes more easily in a mansion full of weapons.

Big Data, border control and mannequins with projection of Donald Trump's face.

Same as it ever was...

Same as it ever was... Same as it ever was...

Same as it ever was... Same as it ever was... Same as it ever was...

Beach me.

Feine Leute.

Url up and die.

La Vie Ignoble.

Love is in the air.

Anonymity is over.

Science and magic.

See yourself sensing.

Faith No More: Easy.

Breaking the borders.

Pigging out in Samoa.

Cruyff Is In The Heart!

Do apes have churches?

NO CASH – Cards Only.

Privacy is a human right.

e be to him who thinks e.

Clocking in, clocking out.

Nothing seek, nothing find.

The Boatman's Call is mine.

The Underground Mail-Agent.

The Left-To-Die-Boatman's Call.

La solitude vivifie, l'isolement tue.

The river Styx we all have to cross.

I'm going to teach you how to Cruz!

Men, boats, animals and computers.

Pretty pennies are ugly by definition.

Hyper-inflating the mind of the world.

Cutting out the deadwood everywhere.

We are being datafied big time, people!

Down the robot-hole we fall and drown.

Only the miracle of love can save us now.

Our identity has become partially digital.

Invisible Friend (will text you right back!).

I had to phone someone so I picked on you.

Kienholz: The State Surveillance Hospital.

Colour TV 1940, Prozac 1987, Youtube 2005.

Winged gods walking on MacAir wordy-widy.

Codes, lines, walls, screens, borders, passwords.

Tim getting out of Bill's pool (2 men in a shower).

Prince Ratohep Gates and his wife Nofret Melissa.

All Gods Children: The Tim Cook Cult Experience.

Not everything is being made visible in the same way.

Ron L. Vox & U2 Jive8 Jazzmafezz Big Band: Vanilla Sky.

People, goods, bisons, capital, information, schizophrenia.

I prefer my love-life to be analogue if you really wanna know.

That nothing really matters, and most things don't matter at all.

So social media and societal scar tissue blotted by Bill Gates' lipstick.

Flowers between the toes of your loved one, nothing more and just that is that.

Infected.

Compare.

Tikipedia.

Learn more.

Coming soon.

Let's go to bed.

Lumia 950 BC.

Out of Control?

Watch The Med.

I Hung My Head.

Seen And Not Seen.

Ted Can Cruzzifix It!

iLife During Wartime.

Slave to the Algorithm.

The Nemesis Machine.

Contesting testing, 1, 2.

Fabrication Américaine.

iShell, McEsso, BP King.

Zippin' the ol' Cala Loco.

What did you e last night?

The Cure: Play For Today.

Leave your laptop at work.

Hotel! Motel! Holiday Inn!

Microsoftcell: Tainted Love.

Turn inspiration into action.

Rich capture of bitter poverty.

Take a lickin' and keep trickin'.

I didn't have the nerve to say no.

Ricard Dixan's Watergate Down.

It's the Lumia you have been waiting for.

See all accessories, view all specifications.

A nice bit of Bush bashing, who can resist it?

Banks, bisons, governments, multinationals.

iBurger McCoca Cola King Kong HeinZAPP!

Porky & Bass (Pulled Porky & Plucked Bass).

Sly & The Family Stone H: Fresh Out of Hell.

(I'm Always Touched By Your) Presence, Dear.

Mr. Jones... Grace Jones, God Bless Grace Jones!

Connect your anteater to a Microsoft Display Dock.

Wifi Cody & The Bison Testicle All-Stars: Sweet Home Alabama.

Discover the HH tour circuit circus by downloading the free MMA App.

Unleash the potential of your digital life with a stunning Quad HD Display.

Are you gonna go my way? Are you gonna go your way? Are we gonna go our way?

@=mc².

ZZ GOP.

Digital Abendrot.

Photography is dead.

Here we are nowhere.

This Is What We Find.

Man, Myth, Microsoft.

Moulding mud is back.

Living in the real world.

The Natives Are Restless.

Nivea Men starts with you!

Lost in the supermarket of e.

Nasadisiacs for space junkies.

This is not the way of the world.

We just downloaded each other.

Technology is going way too fast.

Tandy Warhol Radio Snack 1992.

Siberians prefer snow to hotlines.

While I commit my social suicide.

William 'Biggus Diggus' Gates III.

Khloe Kardashian: Tight & Mighty.

Psychedelics for the middle classes.

Flip to play, play to win, win to loose.

GOP-Art, GOP-Music, GOP-Culture.

Powered by Life – Sponsored by Nature.

Water dissolving... and water removing...

Villa Borges: The Book of Imaginary Bisons.

Thin Ziggy: The Coyote Calls (Fame Remix).

Facebook: The Phenomenology of Delusions.

Welcome to the XS4ALLSDSMisney World War 3!

We have pictures of Mick Jagger but not of Heraclitus.

DSM-666 and Navaho classification of natural objects.

Avant-Robotic Humanity, White-Washington DC and cartoonic-cloonic clandestinos.

Yes We Can't!

Coca Coahuila.

My aim is true.

Do (not) despair.

The Desire Machine.

Whining in the Dark.

Widen your wor(l)d(s).

Streaming my life away.

Microsoft Lumiagara Falls.

Beanz! Beanz! Beanz! Beanz!

Dalai Lemmy: Age of Spades.

Celebrate the bullet, Armorica.

Calais Cauchemar: Jungle People.

Digital variables and virtual constants.

Bitch better have money, I'm Madonna.

All e is fated to become the new Atlantis.

Loonie Riefenstahl's Trumph des Willies.

I'm sure you care, Terry Ted (Cruz 2016).

We are the Sultans... the Sultans of Bling...

Melissa Gutz: A Good Heart Is Hard To Find.

The flakes reminded me of you, Megyn Kellogg's!

Philanthropy is too much money in a guilty heart.

Jeff Bozzio & Amazappazon All-Stars: Rat Tomago.

Macbook Proust: A La Recherche Du Temps Perdu.

The eradication of Polio Psycho Pop is the real challenge.

Daddy Dadalai Lenny Cool: I Love The Smell Of Nepal In The Morning.

Welcome To Sioux City (Where The American Popcorn Company Resides).

Strawberry Spangled Banner: 1 l. Martini Rosato, 4 l. strawberry juice, Downfrost HD Fluid.

Applocalypse Now!

Down in the dumps of e.

Bill does not cut the mustard.

The Google Glass of Absinthe.

1936: Tim, the speaking clock.

Billy Goat and Tree (Ur, 2600 BC).

Never let your minds be colonized.

www: The Darktown Strutters' Ball.

After you get what you want, Swanee.

In Bill Gates' Syncopated Bob Cats Band.

The calculated destruction of Men's Minds.

Thinking online or the tragedy of clicktivism.

If you want to know all about Bill, ask a priest.

I feel alone even when there are people around.

Billy Willy, the Leaping Internet Mountain Goat.

Eagle-trapping, privacy, transparency, surveillance.

Nocturne in Black and Gold: The Falling Rocket of e.

Dionysos Today – grapes, dolphins and body scanners.

Bill Gates wears what he wants to wear (and that's it!).

On the Fossil Human Skull recently discovered online.

The Laestrygonians hurling rocks at the fleet of Captain Tim Cook.

For The Love of Manet: The Naked Luncheon on the Leaves of Grass.

iChing, Tarot 'n roll, ESP SIMcards, Big Astrodata, erzatz voodoo curses.

Black & White America: Mae & Kanye West are one and the same person.

Accessible writing, mouse terminology and modern Microsoft death event.

A popular selection of Ethiopian serenades as sung at the launch of iPhone6.

Ev'rybody's Crazy 'Bout the Eagle Coin-Slot Graphophone But I'm Not Happy.

The immanent birth of a kitsch buffalo skull in the terrarium of the world-elite.

Computers in the classroom: The schools we need and why we don't have them.

Thelonious Monkey Mouse & Walt Dixieland Jazz S.O.S. Band: Don't blame me.

Dwelling in the earth, in rivers and lakes, in the rain, in sun and moon, not the internet.

I Agree.

YankTank.

Start free trial.

Microsoft Got Style!

Get Grammarly Now!

Wearing our bitmasks.

High-level language, yes?

Read between these lines.

The stampeding herds of e.

Wasting time, and lots of it.

Hitting the mail on the head.

Wordwrapping hologrammar.

Domesticating (a) wilderness.

Talking the legs of an iron iPod.

Watch yourself, you're goin' down.

Under My Wings Everything Prospers.

Into the Gym of Obsolete Technologies.

Microsoft: We Want To Hear From You.

Clicking through your garbage collection.

There is water at the bottom of the ocean.

Push the cancel button whenever you see one.

Time zones, Zip Codes and online clairvoyance.

Machine language syntax in the New-Found Land.

A verbal reproduction of my 1st painting on iPad Pro.

I'm a memory-resident of this world (and I didn't know).

Flat out like a lizard drinking absinthe from a Google glass.

Code examples, command syntax and bison-skin tepee-fonk.

iBeam, Gotcha4, Hot Link, Gypsy Moth, groupware, Big Bone Lick.

Pia Kjaersgaard & Danish State Radio Symphony Orchestra: Stand and Deliver!

Setting me up.

Now is too late!

The Evil iPhone.

Life on your screen.

La machine égalitaire.

River spirits swing low.

Turn me on, turn me off.

Life Hack & Death Control.

Down to the waterline of love.

How children think and learn.

The Cure: Staring At The Zoo.

Gossip till gossip exhausts itself.

Online the flying saucers are real.

Constant connectivity is a problem.

The offline breakthrough to creativity.

Dr. John Major: Gris-gris, gumbo ya-ya!

USA: OFF THEIR ROCKER since 1789.

New illiteracy for a non-diverse society.

The Birdfeather Astrological Space e-Book.

www or the case of the psychic energy field.

High tech and low life live in the same world.

e-learning with Carlos Castaneda, lazy and gents.

T-Mail – a telepathic dream across the nation states.

Madness may be breakthrough as well as breakdown.

Your PC: The Brain Wave Synchronizer Self-Hypnosis Machine.

...as the inner world overwhelms our structured ego images online...

Escape from Microsoft (A Definite History of the Penitentiary Years).

Civil disobedience, holographic technology and Linda Goodman's Sun Signs.

Fried Microsoft-ice Is A Reality, all over the world man (Dannatt not Hofstede).

Badge of Honor: 1 oz. Pucker Lemonade Lust Vodka, 3 oz. Club Soda, ½ oz. sulphuric acid.

The Cloud.

Mental Radio.

That's an error.

Music to smile by.

The Film Sense, lost.

Fortune by numbers.

On Grief and Reason.

The risks of software.

The Digital Sandwich.

A bomb waiting to explode.

Understanding catastrophe.

Go the whole world wide way!

Not one sea-dog knows Bill's address.

Is the brain's mind a computer program?

Carry the water at the bottom of the ocean.

God's rights, man's rights, machines' rights.

Computers in the classroom (ADHD-DAY).

Then, with his fingers, Bill sowed a tear into it.

Sometimes the past says more about the present.

Imagination, humanity and love expressed in money.

There's not much you can do against a nuclear disposition.

eWitches burnt at modern One Microsoft Way death event.

The Information Highway: We're On The Road To Nowhere.

The Tim Cockatook Bird Monument for MacAirspace travellers.

Alpha brain waves, artificial intelligent life and oneiro-imagologies.

Roto-Relief, Optophonetics, Anémic Cinema and the spirit of opposition.

Sir Stern/Ernst Ris ft. The Poprise Snake-Charmer All-Stars: Don't Speak.

Let's keep body and soul together, you, me, and all our friends, offline & elsewhere.

The Internet has changed the child from an irresistable force to an immovable object.

Close to you.

Pictures of you.

Crying one's e out.

Let our children go!

Chacun son paradis.

A PC-like experience.

Let your hair down, America.

Zickie (Cheney) played guitar.

Mein Trumpf 2: The Fall of the Wall.

The Great American Digital Sermon.

We're Gonna Have James Marshall Law!

One day sooner than later we'll laugh again.

Contesting testing technological border control.

Electronic phantasmagoria for the middle classes.

Throwing up daily in the Apple Career Path Program.
Gnomeland security, necromancy and psychic attack.
Roll me over and let me go (Running free with the buffalo).
A Razor for Billy Willy, the leaping Internet Mountain Goat.
www: Aleister in Wonderland (Black Crowley Armorica Remix).
Brat Depp & Lollywood Tuxedo Onward Brass Band: Men in Black.
Transmuting the post-industrial lives we live alone and with others.
Sleeping on a pile of rotting livers, somewhere on the Internet Mountain.
The Void.
I ShoPPP.
I Go Wild.
Phone it in.
Real People.
The Crack Up.
Rat On The Run.
See full schedule.
Not Now (Allow).
A Game of Dwarfs.
Occupied territory.
Spamspung forever.
Hooked on a feeling.
Prepaid afterparties.
Mind your language.
The weakness in me.
Show some emotion.
Time will pass you by.
We're too young to die.
Select, sling and shoot.
Shot into designer space.
The Cloud of Inner Speech.
Television: Marquee Moon.
Van GO with the DADA-flow!
Free to succeed, bound to fail.
Pay your bills from anywhere.
Keep me locked out, I beg you.
Sir Hillary is only partly human.
Portable storage for the paranoid.
Have something to say about this?
Of trash and spam and sea-urchins.

Shopping errors in the virtual body.

I don't eat from your manual, sorry!

The Tartaros Sandwich Machine Part 11.

Dongles, MiFi, Tablets and Bird Fossiles.

Schizoid bastards behind scruffy screens.

Jay Zuckerburger's Tidal Wave of Money.

Disney wants your soul, mind and money.

Computers won't work in the next Ice-Age.

He has become an irregular sleep/wake type.

Rewriting Warhol: The Brillo Soup Disasters.

Mandrill: Chain on your heals like (a) stone man.

Just plug in and play anything, anytime, anywhere.

Apple: The Linguistic and Behavorial Implications.

Tornados, hacks, hurricanes, bugs, blizzards, worms.

Hand flapping, body rocking, head banging, self-biting.

Status for remote access is what asylum-seekers know.

Web-surfing and developmental coordination disorder.

Clear: The Hooloch Barry Gibbon YMCA-Bomb The Bass.

Presidential elections, Hyperdrive and Acute Stress Disorder.

Joseph Campbell's Hugo Ballroom Blitzoup... hot and delicious!

McHabsburger King Monarchs, spirit possession and schizophrenia.

Bison habitat destruction and biomedical diagnosis and treatment of depression.

Near-extinction of bison and planned reintroduction of herds in Manhattan for 2018.

Don't believe a word they tell you, them, us, him, her or the Genus Ping Pongo Orangutans.

Compose.

How do I...?

Read my mind.

Sick and wired.

All About Spam.

Please try again.

Baby Come Back.

Experience more.

Find more friends.

Band Of Monsters.

Smoking fiberglass.

Life Worth Dying For.

The future of our eyes.

I loved the phonebook.

Obsessive/Compulsive.

48

Game of Thrones: Genesis.

State of the World Address.

All the President's Manners.

BlackBerry White of course...

Barbara Bush: Read my labia.

Popular in your network today.

You're not the only one I know.

Going blind as a Bat Out Of Hell.

Show the world what you can do.

Virtual artifice and cult totemism.

My cyber-optic breakfast, every day.

Video alerts, bible alerts, astrology alerts.

The Internet... a global voyeuristic disorder.

Something is not always better than nothing.

AXIOMERICA: Material | Rap Is Still An Art.

Vodafone Mumbai (First we take Manhattan...).

Smokie On The Water: Living Next Door To LSD.

Cornflakes, iPhones, Honey Pops, Google glasses.

US traumatologists provoking traumas, what else?

There ain't a problem that I can't fix, cos' I can do it in the mix.

Uncle Jamiroquai or The White Barry Gibbonline Species Cowboy.

Press here.

Out of focus.

Roger? Roger?

Flasher Player.

In Zipperspace.

Zen, chip, water.

Loosing our minds.

Out offline, out of mind.

The Absence of the Real.

Change the way you play.

To get with which program?

The man who sold the earth.

If money is the food of love...

We gotta get out of this place.

Money is running out of ideas.

Collecting shells and bones, I remember.

Bicycle... bicycle... I want to ride my bicycle!

Dreams, nature, drums, waters, money, 7UP.

Where theres a fork, a knife is never far away.

Dr. Dr. MabUsenetwork that body body body!

We apparently all have the right to have rights.

The Virtual Kaleidoscope of Proletarian Celebrity.

The Silicon Valley Man: rhinos, winos and lunatics.

Il n'y a pas de mystères ce qui concerne l'ordinateur.

You don't have to believe in Funk Shui for it to work.

From gaming to droning to plain, fast forward murder.

A vibrant depiction of the creative power we have... ah, forget it!

Selling anything to anyone at any given moment, for any shameless price.

Apple, Coca-Cola, Starbucks, Beats By Dre, Carlyle Group, Bank Of America.

In the dark.

Such is life not.

Bits of Freedom?

Stolen generation.

Spitting the dummy.

The Homeless Mind.

Who is to be believed?

Like a shag on the rock.

Calling Tim Cook's bluff.

Kustom Kar Kommando.

Living to tell the tale of e.

3D-printing my after-life.

Making no bones about IT.

Alienation, isolation, deprivation.

I'm feeling very emojinal right now.

Race, power, control and resistance.

A selfie of a bulldog chewing a wasp.

The US is getting away with murder.

Lady Dianetics vs. Lady Illuminagaga.

I didn't come down in the last shower.

Bill Gatecrashing the end of the world.

The sun doesn't shine online, simply simple.

The electronic pursuit of the 3rd Millennium.

The passage from fire to water is not an easy one.

Welcome to the Deaths-At-The-Border-Database.

Online Man, and his anxiety to penetrate futurity.

Living digital constraint in the remote control society.

The eager beavers of the Californian innovation nation.

I got Bird's custard dripping from my eyes, hitchhiking on the Internet Mountain.

Liberty Belle Mojito: 1 750 ml. bottle of Bacardi, 2 l. Mojito mix, 6 oz. friction reducer.

Getaway.

Write-only.

Where is Dad?

Al Jarreau: Spirit.

Going to the dogs.

Colouring the news.

Kilowatt per second.

The Hidden Seducers.

Where did our love go?

No more sense of place.

Language, image, media.

MIP Mapping El Mundo.

The seashore of endless worlds.

Twitter: Here Comes Everybody.

Love, devotion and show business.

Sand between your toes... the best!

Programmers and deprogrammers.

Apple is a Unificationist movement.

It's up to you not to heed the call-up.

Korean freedom is none of our business.

Bird feathers, Readme files and release notes.

You know that they know, but they don't know what you know.

Are you ready?

Email intuition...

We No Who U R.

Sing a simple song.

Crazy Like (The) US.

When you gonna learn?

See You Later Navigator!

ZzzzzzzzzzzuckerBEURK!

Make Microsoft Great Again.

Masturbation is a monologue.

Byte worming its way into being.

You drag and drop the bomb on me.

Home away from home on the Mac.

Bone-tired from the mental onslaught.

Sometimes I feel I don't have a partner.

Daydreaming and Beyoncé Ivy Park adds.

Offlineness, innocence and the Good Life.

Cosmetic Consciousness: Eternal Freedom.

35% of all internet downloads are pornographic.

iCal-girls will change your Microsoft Outlook on life.

The long-range effect of our onlineness is truly unknown.

Someone please, get me David Lee Roth on the telephone.

The Internet is influencing mental health across the globe.

Get your facts first, then you can distort them as you please.

Internet, recession, anxiety, sleeplessness, constant worrying.

It's worth stumping up the extra cash for Microsoft Office Erotics.

McMick Jaggerwocky: Microsoft Windows 95 Video Launch – Start Me Up.

I may be drunk, Madonna, but in the morning I will be sober and you will still be ugly.

King of Candy Zuckerburger & Shakin' Steven Hawkins: Whole Lotta Shakin' Goin' On.

Sgt. Ginger e Fred Hot Heinz Jelly Beanz Prepper's Loonie Arts Club Mad: Sir Psycho Sexy.

Pricy.

DNSA.

Once More?

Wolves-a-go-go.

Virtual Insanity.

Spend a lifetime.

Material | Mantra.

The American Ego.

Truth or Dare: Lies.

Cannot contain this.

www, Love and God.

Play In The Sunshine.

Proteus Digital Health.

Tweaking The Intertext.

Looking through darkness.

D'ya Accept Tim's Cookies?

Black Mozart – Blue Rimbaud.

Connectivity benefits everyone?

You may delay, but time will not.

In drag and dropping the bomb on e.

It's an unhappy ducksoup all together.

O Lord, help me to be pure, but not yet.

Walt 'Whitman' Disney: Leaves of Mouse.

All of us and offline elimination of suffering.

Living out da funk in a robotic surgery suite.

Drinks On The Go at the Apple Formula Bar.

Digital psychosis and multipharma solutions.

Minotauring the heartbeats of the age we live in.

Billy 'Gates' Graham and the vision of an Ideal World.

A Universal Injustice: The sun also shines on assholes.

The day Barack Obama will realise he is in fact Al Green.

Roses are red, violets are blue, I'm schizophrenic, and so am I.

Microsoft media essentials and Didjerama Digital Vibrations.

A celebrity perfume is the battery-acid of Pop-Consciousness.

Cosmic intelligence and the ephemeral e-knowledge explosion.

AXIOMERICA: Various | Axiom – Reconstructions & Vexations.

Donny Trumpadelic & The Grand Old Funk Combover Combo: Crazy Horses.

In the 20s, the world's virtual population will outnumber the population of the Earth.

Lady Gaga, Miley Cyrus, Paris Hilton, Britney Spears & The Human Potential Movement.

The Anti-Christiano Ronaldo McDonaldo & L'Oréal Madrid Magic Blur Revitalift Laser X3.

Bio-feedback, Starbucks Coffee nerves and e-idolatry discouraged by Maharishi Mahesi Yogi.

Notify me.

Don't Do It!

Cowboy Song.

Shuttershocked.

Next to nothing.

Bloody Tourists.

Dissinfordollars.

#ComeTogether.

How Dare You 2!

Billy 'Jean' Gates.

In Good We Trust.

Nature is a language.

A Fool Not Like Him.

We're glad you're here.

End digital serfdom now.

Looking forward in anger.

Let's take the scenic route!

A robot aims for the moon.

Masculinity is a monologue.

Collect moments not things.

You Can't Fool The Fat Man.

Scrolling down memory lane.

Apple | Hermès: Cold Fusion.

Keep your eye on the sparrow.

New at Mc: The Bowel Burger.

Lost time is never found again.

Mumia, What's A Trumpadelic?

Download The We Fashion App.

I love America and America loves me.

Online voyeurism, terms and privacy.

The Nuclear G-Spotify Premiumbrella.

And I think we got it all wrong anyway.

Essentially Anti-Nature is What I.T. Is.

Emoji, Teletubbies, Imbeciles, Jellybabies.

The robot gets fat on what the hare misses.

Returning to the Place of No Development.

Public perceptions are never left to chance.

Don't roll the dice if you can't pay the price...

There's a sad feeling growing over our heads.

3rd Disney-World Wars: The Jungle Facebook.

Ancestors and tree spirits, be funking, like George.

20 million songs and unable to decide what to listen to.

Gaming is your principle discipline at Drone University.

The West's War against African development continues.

Brothas! Sistas! We Don't Need This Fascist Groove Thang!

And the green parrots of Amsterdam still love John Lennon.

Africom, proxy music wars and global internet propagandada.

Today's forecast: cloudy with a chance of purple rain (210416).

The Information Infrastructure and Funkhansaplast Universal.

How to read Donald Duck: Imperialist Ideology in the Disney comic.

Rudolf Funkensteiner & The Saint Tropezophical Society: Hotel California.

Davy Becker, John Calvin Klein and the Posh Spice Chili Preppers on Cloud 777.

Zooming in on a metaphysical epiphany through the lens of a surveillance camera.

We abstain.

Along the way.

The Gospel of e.

Abbottabad Road.

If you can't say no.

Everything is wrong.

F/rigidity is hip girls!

Diamonds and pearls.

As long as you PayPal!

How extremely stupid.

Welcome to Hard Times.

Schubert is real medicine.

Dead Men Trick No iTools.

What the birds say about e.

This is the sign of the times.

Guaranteed (Into The Wild).

I remember writing by hand.

Navigators destroy intuition.

7 billion people can be wrong.

Even robots insult a dead lion.

New friends, new faces, places!

You make me feel mighty real...

The Donald: Shock The Monkey.

Prozac killings and Wifi shootings.

www: All that met thine infant eye.

Charity is a monologue about guilt.

Bill, Auf Wiedersehen Motherfucker!

L. Ron and RAM will wait for no man.

Reading The Brangelina Times online.

One day the www will be a digital ruin.

L'homme virtuel du Mammouth à Spy.

I'm the slime oozing out of your PC set.

Système des ordinateurs sans vertèbres.

The jaw in question is indeed Steve Jobs'.

Internet, anxiety, depressions and glaciers.

Depp! Depp! Depp! Depp! Depp! Depp! Depp!

A Certain Rational Approach To Online Funk.

Bill G: How to vacation with 76 billion dollars.

Rate in burning calories per hour: browsing – 0.

I'm tired of all the negativity that's going round.

The iNeandertools: Changing the image of Man.

For the love of God, RAM, fame and dirty money.

Cloud computing and near-permanent death-data.

In the Paris Hilton Hotel of Hollow Ego Projection.

Femininity is a not a monologue but a conversation.

AXIOMERICANA: Sonny Shamrock | Ask The Ages.

The night Prince kicked Kim Kardashian off the stage.

Listen! Listen to me, and I will breathe into thee a soul!

From Turkish military bands to Spotified iNDIE-Tunes.

Black as the night is black, black like the depths of your Africa.

De La Soul Shadows: 3 Feet High & Rising Global Connectivity.

The Internet or other transitional forms between apes and men.

Black bones, red bones, yellow bones, and, hélas, white bones too.

L. Ronald Reagan: Are You Better Off Than Your Black Neighbour 2?

My baboon went through a devastating Illuminati mind control program.

Prince Charles Darwin & The Silicon City Beat Band: The Origin of sPC's.

Tangiers at the time when William Burroughs managed not to shoot Mick Jagger.

Tim cruising and digital sardines worshipped by Katie Holmes during Spy-Fi childbirth.

Sharing?

Freeeze Out!

Force De Frappe.

Emojinal Rescue.

Je Suis Confused.

Because We Care.

Holland DADATA.

Ma place dans le trafic.

Borders legitimate war.

Data, Drones, Disziplin.

New Golden Dream 2017.

Hypnos is getting restless.

Celebrating the self online.

Who Really Is Atlas Today?

Living a post-internet reality.

Coming In From The Coldplay.

'Who Owns Me?' I'd like to know.

POP, or the infantilization of us all.

Mails, phone calls, movement patterns.

Let's go, let's go for a scroll in the country.

Masculinity is a monologue about femininity.

iApples, homoticons and the Neoliberal news diet.

And watch events unfold, in real time, from every angle.

The blackness of nightmares will turn to gold eventually.

More than SMARTness we need kindness, and gentleness.

A ruined heart is left for the dogs to eat and eat themselves.

Même si l'iPhone a tout pour lui, on peut toujours en rajouter.

Rewriting Warhol: Riding Naomi Campbell Soap-turtles online.

Cocaine Cool Cats, white collar crimes and Superpowder rivalry.

It's not over till the fat lady sings (Madame Calamity Dub Remix).

Fusion, fission, split, roll over Beethoven and bisons, and let me go.

Live8, or the narcissistic attraction to address the suffering of others.

The Dreadful Business of Dance Music: SENSATION – Angels & Demons.

Counting the money: DSM-5, iPhone6, Galaxy Edge S7, Cloud 9, Microsoft OS10.

The Ethernet Anthropozoophoncy Orchestra: We're Only In It For The Astral Money.

Dritte Welt: Massenkommunikation und kolonialisme bei Micky Mouse und Donald Duck.

PC Rider.

All you can e.

The Intersex.

False friends.

Répondez moi.

No Wifi No Cry.

Best in the West.

How Do You Dotube?

Accurate and verified.

Spreading like WiFire.

Categorise your appetites.

USA, USB, USC, USD, USE.

And all this is folly to the world.

Less expensive is what we need.

Water of e, FireWire and Ice Age 3.

Cheap Nokia phones go a long way.

O doleful nerds, and goblins merry!

Let there be commerce between us.

And we all Must See Video all the time.

Storing information in the Stratocumulus.

iPhones growing inside the hearts of children.

Stay on top of your finances by staying offline.

Femininity is a conversation about masculinity.

The Bill & Melinda Loveless Foundation Nation.

Minimalising my privacy and reputation concerns.

Andy Warhol's Jelly Bean Factory – 36 gourmet flavours.

Mind control is what made America great in the first place.

Prehistoric music, internet mania and Cloud Classification.

Poe-Funk: Descending into the Hell of planetary online souls.

As long as humans and not computers are running this world...

Microsoft ODSM-X and the creation of mental illness categories.

Hypertension, L'Oréal Sublime Body and Master Apple's smart asses.

Deep inside the Garden of Eden standing there with my hard-on bleedin'.

Me, my friends and the sex machine (do unto others like my brother bean).

Haptic paralysis, investable health technology and the Van Gogh Syndrome.

Barackless Husseinz & ObamAll Beanz White House Orchestra: Let's get it on.

Still I must take complete responsibility for all my actions both public and private.

iDrop Dead.

Promised land.

Get the stretch!

Amor del Bueno.

Wait, there's more!

Windows and swans.

Designing mediocrity.

Hell has a website too.

Countdown to ecstasy.

Space Invader Infinity.

I was halfway crucified.

Phones, phones, phones.

Marlburroughs Country.

First Bison On The Moon.

The Time Flies Are Coming!

Madonna, spiked and plated.

Don't believe Jurassic World.

Are you with me, Doctor Wu?

Your new name is Blackburn!

The Clash: Career opportunities.

Microsoft Office 3001 A Space Oddity.

How to buy, destroy and sell the world.

Roll me over and let me go, riding in the rodeo.

Do This Now To Keep Your Brain From Shrinking Later.

Six hundred unknown heroes were killed like sleeping buffalo.

'Rock n' Roll doesn't mean being bad at business.' Bono Christ.

Kill Bill.

Kill Bill 2.

Feelings...

As You Like It.

No Es Normal.

Hate Unlimited.

Building happiness.

Are we in a river lost?

Apology for Duckology.

The song is too familiar.

Mariosoft Lumaca 1970.

Fotografie und Kreativität.

Heroes keep walking in Hell.

What you see is what you will.

Making more waste from waste.

The astral projection of e is futile.

Don't come closer or I'll have to go.

Manage your transgenfers smarter.

From Chaos is born a dancing light.

Lizard-tailored to move: Rafael Nada.

Slinging bones in the age of Unreason.

The human use/abuse of human beings.

You don't need a computer to show ideas.

Hot, Cool and the Brainless Involvement.

We must listen to the voices that seem useless.

Fast food for slow minds | slow food for fast minds.

By using our services, you agree to our Cookie Use.

Nowhere the cash is flowing like in the IT industry.

Internet, Marxism and the problem of tech-linguistics.

Les mythes sont faits pour que l'imagination les anime.

Rewriting Warhol: Electric Red and Blue Rietveld Chair.

Trending Now: iPad Pro, Johnny Depp, ADHD treatment.

Connect with your friends – and other fascinating people.

Donald L'Imposteur ou l'Impérialisme raconté aux enfants.

Ever read of that greatgrand landfather of our visionbuilders?

Empire State Surveillance and McWrap Pull Porkafied misery.

Accessoires Apples. Redessinés. Rechargeables. Remarquables.

Cropping the image of Man and the failure to achieve world peace.

Get in-the-moment-updates on all the things you find uninteresting.

Pollution de la nature! Decomposition de l'humanité! La fin du monde!

Ronald McDonald Duck, McStarbucks Zuckerburgers, Mäuse und Tastaturen.

Lipton Ice Tea and Royal Greenland Pizza Hut miseries not based on mind's nature.

Franky Interstella, Rocky Rauschenberger and Michael Jacksonian Pollock epilepsy.

I don't see why I should give my new music to iTunes or anyone else (Prince Roger Nelson).

Yesterday.

Card, Pin, Cash, Ass.

Pure Pleasure Seeker.

USA: Simply The Best.

(You Caught Me) Smilin'.

The worst of both worlds.

Everywhere and nowhere.

Travelling without moving.

Somebody's Watching You.

Sometimes it snows in April.

Visionquest for a better world.

Distraction-free writing at its best.

What kind of person is Bono Christ?

The Lost Children (Michael Jackson).

The US is a monologue about the world.

All this is that and all that was yesterday.

Paris Hilton: I swatted her like no SWAT team can.

USAXIOMERICA: Bahia Black | The Seven Powers.

Internet dating and post traumatic bitterness disorder.

American culture is a dominant force at home and abroad.

Microsoft, devotion, direction and Paleo personal progress.

Fracture: Barack Obama, the Clintons and the racial divide.

Pøp-Upszide down und aus come da freaksz, da nerdsz, da geeksz!

'Microsoft Mon Amour is my favorite bathroom bluff.' Oprah Winfrey.

The tragedy of online knowledge not prescribed by Maharishi Mareshi Yogi.

Universal love, Transcendental Superstition and Microsoft White Power Peak experiences.

Still Bill.

Emancipation.

Sheep thought I.

Tell Your Friends!

Give Us Feedback!

iPhones Wide Shut.

Gadgets and fossiles.

The evolution of type.

Choose Your Language.

Time passes irrevocably.

Beyond Good and Email.

Sign in to confirm your H.

Some people gotta have it...

The Internet: Your Portrait.

Ridge Over Troubled Water.

And the world will be as one.

Al Green: Tired of being alone.

We'll need you to do this today.

We are made of atoms and bits.

Microsoft Bulumia Nervosa 950.

Drilling holes in the walls of Hell.

Ashcroft to Ashcroft, dust to dust.

Freedom fries and liberty cabbage.

Time and tide will wait for no man.

Did you read the Statue of Liberty?

Tech Support will answer you now!

Pop or the expulsion from Paradise.

Apple Watch: Folge dem Rhythmus.

But learning is free anyhow, peoples...

You can change this preference below.

Do you know where your children arc?

Que Viva Vivaldi!: 4 Seasons In Heaven.

Burger King: The House of the Habsburger.

Choose your credit rating to estimate pricing.

Who We Are Who Uses Us How We've Helped.

Chat, Skype, text, like, tweet, blog and comment!

Human warmth does not travel fiberglass cables.

The North American Buffalo und Apple Zubehör.

Friends! Friends! Friends! I have so many friends!

The Power of Equality is not yet what it ought to be.

LSDSM-5 Diagnosis via POP3 and IMAP4 protocols.

The New World Grand Funk Internet Disorder Circus.

Sharing news and tips from the Gmail team and friends.

Microsoft Mon Amour: A line a day keeps the doctor away.

www.applestore.comuniacion masiva y revolucion socialista.

Cyclothymic internet visits and Web-induced mood disorder.

To be mentally elsewhere, all the time, is not good for anybody.

Hello there! I'm McMicky Logitech MX Anywhere 2 Wireless Maus!

Fred Flipkart & The Indian Digital Buyers Penetration Nation: Money...

Aw!... You Great Bolshy Yarblockos! You're viewing Youtube in English!

It's the so-called healthy that have brought the world to the verge of ruin.

Ted Cruz & The Brides of Funkenstein: Never Buy Texas From A Cowboy.

No such thing as spare time, free time, down time, all you got is life time, go!

Trending Now: LG G5, David Bowie, Sarah Palin and Weight Loss programs.

We must fill our eyes and ears with things that are the beginning of a great dream.

Bewitched, bothered, sunburnt and bewildered and lonely as the child inside my eyes.

Quaffoff Tim Cook's fraudstuff and sink teeth through that path of his flowerwhite bodey.

Getting by.

Unwatched.

Unspecified.

Let's talk type!

My life in design.

Maniac Mansion.

Find your signature.

Turn your wifi low...

Shout!... let it all out...

Mappa Mundi Mania.

After the thrill is gone.

Trump is a borderliner.

I am in the mood again!

NSA, NRA, NWA, NBA.

We are friends on Facelift.

Your Self Adhesive Future.

The Last Days of Microsoft.

Staring at my screen forever.

Conmen, Commen, Common.

You're most webcam, Madame!

Eagles eating snakes... Mexico...

Outkast: Happy Valentine's Day.

The Essential Mozart minus one.

Microsoft and hippie modernism.

BT-Mobile sandwiches for digibetics.

Catatonia associated with computing.

SMS, CNN, ABC, LSD, DNA, NSA, NRA.

64 Shots: Crazy leaders in a crazy world.

Chaka Kahn: Scroll Me Through The Rushes.

Private islands for public assholes part 1-2-3.

Ping, Perl, Pentium, P-Funk, Python, Picadon.

Everyone has a song. God gives us each a song.

It had something to do with the telling of Time.

You have drunk the poison firewater from the White Man.

Vamos a la playa – A mi me gusta bailar el ritmo de la noche Donaldo!

Melania Trump: A sweet transvestite from Transsexual Transylvania.

Comandante Marcos Miller ft. Subcomandante Marcos King: Love Games (A Bass Fiesta).

THOR.

Planet Telex.

Ride To Hell.

How are you?

Break a habit.

Koonsifying Life.

I might be wrong.

3 tablet PC's daily.

Eight days a week.

The Ball Street Blitz.

Are you XPerienced?

Sync your highlights.

Hard To Concentrate.

Dismantling virtuality.

Whose side are you on?

Sitting on a cornflake...

The Law of Lotus Software.

Money talks, bullshit walks.

If you don't know me by now.

Top stories just picked for you.

Bill Gates is Number One again!

Oh yes, the Twilight Zone again.

Flash Memory provokes epilepsy.

iSalute Suspicious Activity Report.

The Cruzzifiction of everything Ted.

Don't stop thinking about tomorrow!

HP means psychiatric hospital in French.

Bono Christ hates corruption and injustice.

The unbearable weight of being online 24/7.

Paleo Psycho Pop: Stone Age versus Electronics.

Back in the day: Ted Cruising San Fransisco Bay.

Every generation is known for something indeed.

Joan Armatrading: From The Bottom To The Top.

Surviving on bison livers in the world of the Deepnet.

Bono Christ: The creative punch of big idea branding.

Advancing stadium-rock, mental obesity and terrorism.

Guns n' Roses, Ghosts n' Goblins, Diamond Dogs & Geezers.

Computer talk: reduction of language, and destruction of soul.

3rd World-Warkanoid Android Apps for printing patient-groups.

Valentine!, our feelings have reached consensus, you're irresistible!

Rewriting Warhol: The Jolly Campbell's Mesozoic Soup Can Series.

DNA Registration, manuals, blowjobs, specifications and inside jobs.

Tribal World Wars: The Windows OS 10 vs. The Doors of Perception.

Bono Christ: What I sing is not mine, but belongs to Him who sent me.

George WWW. Bush, a 100 black babies running from his genocidal jaw...

Owl-Faced Monkey traversing the internet with nocturnal autism spectrum disorder.

Wired.

Just Eat.

Go Green.

Silicon Death.

Machine Hell.

Do It Yourself.

A Crazy Man 2.

Dressed to Bill.

Stop this world.

Need For Speed.

Show All History.

Moment Of Heck.

Reinventing Eden.

Better world for kids.

Speaking of Polaroids.

Recommended for you.

It ain't easy to be green.

Ted and Tom, Cruizzified.

Do more with your phone.

Stay with me, speak to me.

I don't need this pressure on.

Internal, global, stable, addicted.

The Great Denial (Clear History II).

Voodoofone: Mounting the Internet.

Rise Of Nations: Thrones and Patriots.

The tide is high (and we're moving on).

Pro Snap Case / The Return of the Madman.

Prepaid and postpaid don't amount to the same.

Apple, Fruit Ninja, Few Days Left, Alien Zombie Dead.

Frogs, careers, spiders, smartphones, lizards, the future.

Unwashed, wired up and somewhere slightly dazed and dizzy.

Get even.

Duplicate All.

Avoid the funk.

Life in the Mac Zone.

Christ, Luther, Gates.

Japan: Visions of China.

Hands across America online.

Paleolithic, Byzantine, Digital.

Sometimes a PC is just in the way.

Now. Easy. Always. Forever. CREATE.

In Nature, butterflies are the real hackers.

The Kumbha Mela is a real collective experience.

Raptors, rockstars, Dino birds and ornithomimids.

Your History Palette is rather revisionist as expected.

Reducing 'Third World' complexity to the comfort of an easy slogan.

Dreamt of Mahatma Gandhi crawling out of a big bed, no, I mean, egg.

Warkanoid IV, Looney iTunes, Drill Sergeant Mindstrong, Crash Bash.

Steamy Windows 10 ISO, Hellmann's Light Mayonnaise and Hellborg's Thumb Basics.

MURPH!

ChaOS X.

What it is.

Do it again.

Get kicking.

iBangladesh.

RIP The Book.

Auto Da Funk.

Stocks to watch.

Compare prices.

The Disconnected.

Middle of Nowhere.

The peace to write...

Knock Knock Nokia.

ZAPPa: Joe's iGarage.

Art For Artaud's Sake!

Gaming, porn, murder.

Reptiles and anonymity.

Bring all to the frontline!

Scanning my limitations.

Today I walk the Red Road.

In Ireland we all have guns.

A fireplace... nothing like it.

Télécharge your intravision.

Brownies, cookies, pancakes.

Coming out of the web-closet.

Shoot that person (an e-mail).

On The Paranoid World View.

This time the girl is gonna stay.

Between web and rock art sites.

The man with the child in his eyes.

No thanks, I'd rather pay full price.

Drag queens to the left if necessary.

Short people have no reason to live...

A sunken Web-city makes no Atlantis.

There ain't no closing time around here.

iRoadmovie + Redux Deluxe (that's all fine!).

Mad World.

No way out.

Where to buy.

Hang 'm High!

iPin, iPen, iPun.

Feel like doin' it.

In a Cyberstorm.

Lonesome Street.

Serpentine water.

Biting the bitcoin.

Shove it, seriously.

Perform Quick Scan.

Kravitz: Lenny Lane.

Beyond the invisible.

Money has a mantra.

Tell us your sun sign.

You are not machines!

Oh! You Pretty Things.

Do not believe in Time.

Dare to live your dreams.

Become the ultimate fan.

Enjoyed these hairstyles?

Introducing the #Cashtag.

Read the f* manual (I did).
Adam's first bank-account.
The bulimia of being online.
Tics, tricks, truffes, torrents.
We have always been wireless.
An eye can think, a lens can not.
Taschen to Taschen, dust to dust.
Big ideas stem from soul inflation.
Type hard if you wanna type faster.
Read More. Read More. Read More.
Ringtones disturb my peace of mind.
One becomes what one displays online.
Michel Foucault: MacBook and Reason.
The Fool On The Hill: Simon Posthuma.
Comanche Indians were there before you.
iTunafish will go extinct before you know it.
Streaming... so much for the live experience.
Here's looking at you, Dionysos Kid Brother.
Happy, wireless, disconnected, free as a bird.
Drumming is the re-enactment of Beginning.
The Magical Mystery Memory Microsoft Tour.
Be the first to know, and the last to understand.
Digital charms to render your husband impotent.
Mummy, my Irises are glued to the bloody screen!
Justin Bieber WDYM Mug € 10.99 (NEW TO STORE).
More than this, through Bono Christ we come to know Jehovah better.
Apple's Diwali Gift: iPhone to arrive in India a week before the festival.
Eagle totem clans, bison secret societies and Elevation board meetings.
In Your Face: White-faced Saki-Monkey staring in the lens of the maniacal unartistic.
Cable love.
Ring my bell.
Ms. Germinator.
Bird on the wire.
Make a statement.
Force quit Reason.
Cleaning Windows.
Let's get out of here!
Meet the new Y-Box.
Murakami in Miami.

Cereal Number Killers.

Is there drive on Mars?

Money back guaranteed.

Leave Page, leave World.

Passports and passwords.

Praying to your disk-icon.

Speed is the trip of the slow.

When an app loves a woman.

The Catwalk of Demi-Reason.

I left my heart in San Fransisco.

Igloo, Pizza Hut, Royal Greenland.

Phoney and the Hardcore: Maggie.

Systematic memory is never poetic.

Mean Girls: High School Showdown.

A waste of space and a waste of time.

Jeb Bush – Hideaway (Official Video).

Microsoft's Definite Guide to Fascism.

The Bullshit Bingo of Online Existence.

Microchips are the dandruff of the dollar.

In retrospect I even liked my supermarket.

In the beginning there was Microsoft Word.

wwwhat the hell do you think you're doing?!

Daddy Don't Live In That New York No More.

Set up other male contacts and calendar accounts.

I achieved the American Dream... and it was awful!

A world population giving way to electronic tyranny.

Firewalls, eating disorders and serpentine blood lines.

Simple Subset Wizard and Dreambox Enigma Disasters.

Elvis Costello & The Attractions: Accidents Will Happen.

Sun spiders, water snakes, bestsellers and clearance sales.

Bird Mimic schizophrenics and 100 recently extinct animals.

Opussy Riot Magnum, mindwash religion, voodoo funk and Art Basel.

Got funk?

Contact Us.

Come again.

Start at home.

Brain Damage.

Write a review.

Come and get it.

Hard to get rid of.
Beliebing In Love.
Staring at a bomb.
Everybody knows.
Back to Buzzcocks.
Secret room service.
A Homepage Prayer.
Machine of the Year.
PRoxy Music Server.
Living my life online.
Lonely at the bottom.
This Time For Africa.
Google Mappa Mundi.
Prepaid and sunburnt.
What shall we ever do?
A song will come to us.
Software is a good cause.
Is there an exit I wonder?
Sindesign for the masses.
Limitation is a good thing.
Riots, ratings and reviews.
That really did me head in.
One broker knows another.
So easy a caveman can do it!
Carry me home to see my kin.
Software for Spider Monkeys.
The Switch, Scream, It's Over.
O Lord, speed me into the lead!
We're gonna get what's coming.
Hacking a joke, cracking a crime.
Mac dust covers make great hats.
My 90-day trial took much longer.
I like the wind and I like the water.
How to switch off defunct printers.
Everybody wants to rule the world.
PC-evangelism and terrorist iTools.
Arizona Wind Spirit Rage Outburst.
Welcome to the Justin Bieber Store.
Onlineness, insomnia and soultravel.

Eating the Apple, peeling the banana.

Flinging my e-smoke into the laqueria.

Come on come on, let's Skype together!

One doesn't sleep under spreadsheets at all.

USB... USB... speaking words of wisdom... USB...

McDonny Trump's Mexican borderline psychosis.

MacAir, Divine Being, Google Glass, Cosmic Mountain.

The Chinese copy everything everywhere anytime anyplace.

Dionysos, Jim Morrison, George Clinton and other Vaudoufone Partygods.

Comandante Che Chuevara ft. Subcomandante Marcos Miller: The Cubass Funk Formula.

Hilarius Clinton & The Brides of Funk-Them-Further: Donald Duck Or Fly! (Ambient Dub).

Robota.

Powerage.

Lowdown.

Que Vera Vera.

Hunting robots.

Such A Woman.

All about robotics.

Coney Island Bison.

Finger Lickin' Good.

The Roaring Silence.

Blondie: Autoamerica.

Lou Reed: Transporter.

T. Rex: Eclectic Warrior.

Gotta... gotta tell the truth.

Life is a cosmic flop... slop...

The horror of hologrammar.

Robots won't know love, ever.

Lately I have been loosing sleep.

Repeat After Me (Blow By Blow).

Minotaurobots will wreck the place.

Who says I've slept with Sarah Palin?

You're once, twice, three times a lady.

U2's evangelical fanbase votes Trump.

Robotic bisons will still kill on instinct.

Knock knock knockin' on Herman's door.

Hollywood Sci-Fi for mediocre mindsets.

We have become aliens to our Mother Earth.

Humanoid robots versus Paranoid Androids.

One shares food not words. ~ Somali Proverb.

The Robotics Institute of American Psychiatry.

The climate and topography of the buffalo habitat.

Hey! I'm going on a robotics summer camp peoples!

Human-robot interaction and the future of rock 'n roll.

Ring the bells that still can ring, forget your perfect offering.

My robot rots into flesh at the foot of the Internet Mountain.

Steely Dan: The Caves of Altamira (Prelude to Stone Age America).

'Trump' reads as 'Wilders' not only when translated by cyber ducks.

The 2016 GOP convention and the extermination of the American Bison.

Popular.

Tutti frutti.

Koyaanisqatsi.

Nice to see you!

Sync your highlights.

Tuttimus | Proximus.

Dismantling virtuality.

Have you met my Wifi?

All you have is your soul.

Bless your hot virgin mouth.

All Image Ready all the time.

Bill Gates' Basic Funk Formula.

We're gonna party like it's 1979!

A disc-driven parrot must be in hell.

Reopen all windows from last sessions.

Connecting with all you psychopaths online.

Digital Beckham voodoo dolls don't sell too well.

Because most hackers turn gamekeepers in the end.

Video gaming, internal/psychotic thought disorder, droning.

The last day of your life... would you spend it surfing the Net?

No Gates No Glory, No Cook No Gladiola, No Jobs No Future.

Tribal World Wars: The Windows OS 10 vs. The Doors of Perception.

Oh my Creator, let me live my song. Let my song honor Your way of life.

Rewriting Warhol: The Jolly Campbell's Mesozoic Soup Cancan Series.

USAXIOM, Bill 'Sanders' Lasworrell and fossil bisons of North America.

Slept well?

Get A Grip.

Save a virgin.

We'll be gone.

Lonely Wölfli.
We are not one.
Hammer to fall.
Je Suis Charlie.
Cut, paste & roll.
Peerless in Gaza.
Addiction to bite.
Talk To Ya Later!
Bieber, done that.
Electro Ladyland.
One Phone Nation.
Where are we now?
Reachability is now.
Planet Google Earth.
After Burner Climax.
Planet, profit, people.
Darkness after Disney.
Monkey see Monkey do.
Anorexia and Lightning.
Tales from the hard side.
Warning (Do Not Enter).
Viruses and worms daily.
No story is ever told online.
Come on baby, bite my wire.
A Quickfix (is what is needed).
I'm in love with Adam Clayton.
Horse sacrifice and photoshop.
Need For Speed 3: Hot Pursuit.
Passion for pioneering the End.
Speed and accuracy don't agree.
Tags, videos, images, categories.
You can't control it, but they can.
The Internet is Otherworld Illusion.
The Apple trees are hung with gold...
Sign up to see what your friends like.
The Plasmatic Wendy Williams Show.
Reopen all windows from last sessions.
The Illusion of Virtual Reality/Insanity.
iCe-Age-3D-Day-Trippin' before the snow.

What to do if your phone or tablet didn't charge.

Dread, online, depression, connected, sick as a dog.

Welcome back if you are back to back to the future is now!

FLOW-MATIC BeanShell & EusLisp Robot Programming.

America and the magic transmutation of the Underworld waters.

TV-evangelism, naming of the bones and formal thought disorder.

Cosmic Snake, soul theft and preemptive MacAirstrikes once again.

Here I am, scrolling down Atlantic Avenue with the sunlight in my eyes.

The death of Obama Bin Laden and the Tibetan mode of the disposal of the dead.

No more time for yourself, or for others, no more being with yourself amongst others.

Bieber's Purpose, Songs of Innocence and otherworld journeys among PC-evangelists.

Desire...

This Is Money.

Have it your way.

The Age of Paranoia.

Billy Bibbit is a robot.

Oops!... I Did It Again.

Ganesha has no email.

I'm deleted to meet you!

Hello from the other side.

Hell! You Need Somebody!

White guys have evil bones.

The Woolworth's Mammoth.

Over and over and over again.

A foul mood is often the result.

Dance is the soundtrack of Hell.

I'm your TripAdvisor (LTSD-25).

Steve Jobs: The jackal-headed god.

Thank you for letting me be your fan.

I'm singing this Jahrhundert to sleep!

I'm your TripAdvisor 2 (LSDSM-25/7).

Sky, like a bowl, and earth, like a desktop.

We are all just robots in the wolf's mouth.

Vincent should have been a jazz musician.

Id, ego, bits, Superman, penises and eagles.

Most birds fly Easyjet going south in winter.

Reading List Items used to be called 'books'.

LSDidipus, digibesitas and born again log-ins.

Taureau Mécanique (Fiesta Latina – Y Mucho Fiesta!)

Lord Shiva wants to get on Facebook (to destroy it all).

Carpool karaoke volumes and elegant bison hip-bones.

AXIOMERICA: Umar Bin Hassan | Be Bop Or Be Dead.

Meatloaf, bison hides and hippie-sprach programming.

Great Spirit, help us to learn and remember the old ways.

Safari Suggestions How To Upgrade Your Miserable Life.

The Virtual Baboon Magic Roadshow Mystery Tour Merch.

The intrinsic boredom of pop-culture yet its capacity to sell itself.

3.366.261.156 internet users on 7.259.902.243 people on the earth.

With a little sacrifice, Jebbin' till the Jeb is through! (Bush Beach McTV Edit).

You have bought guns, knives, kettles from the White Man you can no longer do without.

Be Art.

High e-Tides.

Dunking DPI.

Neander culpa.

Waiting so long.

What's buzzing?

Nothing is great.

Manus Machina.

Become a partner.

It's gonna go away.

Always in my head.

Into the Buffalo Zoo.

Hots on for nowhere.

Utopia's Kindergarten.

Unleash your creativity.

The world is still young.

The torture never stops.

About Vodafone Nigeria.

Welcome to Hard Times.

You shouldn't have bit fish.

Possessing Mother Nature.

The Split Enz of the World.

Seasick, carsick, phonesick.

I Wanna Be Where You Are.

We want more, always more.

Favours, services, exchanges.

A note of the typeface of God.

Restore your (bodily) system.

Classification system of nerds.

A great business idea: Infinity!

Now on MoZillatron FireFox TV!

Fossils, fiberglass and Fang masks.

All the Internet you want, on the go!

Trending Now: The End of the World.

Creating in our own image all the time.

Draw thy iTool... my naked weapon is out.

Edge: An intelligent audience, like MTV's.

Last eWalzheimat for Ronnie MacReggae.

Leeson and gentlemen, Barings my safeties!

Sorcery Saga: Curse Of The Great Curry God.

Hades, depression, Burger King, speech defects.

Beckham Homme Eau de Toilet for Homo Habilis.

Narciso, the new fragrance, available through iTunes.

DSM-5. Mind The Gap – Stay away from closing doors.

Homo Erectus was an evolutionary mistake, obviously.

Joe Bowie's Online Caribbean Rhum and Punch Machine.

Cyber aphasia, animal otherness, Christian slave morality.

Shut the fuck up, Donny! (Make America Great Again 2016).

'Cause I know there is no place like the Avenue when the music gets a hold of you.

Facebook Friends, Night-Monkey Families & The Black Sea Jazz Festival of Fools.

'We should close the American-Dutch border to prevent that sicko from coming in.' Sarah Palin.

Drag.

BASICS.

Off limits.

Delete All.

Uncle RAM.

Slave Driver.

Your Impact.

Lies about IT.

Do Not Disturb.

Monitoring Life.

Personal finance.

Subliminal drive.

Away away away.

Return to sender.

Robocalypse Now!

It's a very deep sea.

Features may vary...
Heaven Help Us All.
Get it while you can.
Abuse Voice Control.
We were all once rain.
River – not databanks.
Damn and be damned.
We do what we're told.
Smile like you mean it.
Life in cartoon motion.
Some kind of madness.
TC Matic Droidcast 43.
When the lights are out.
USA: Suspicious Minds.
He used to cut the grass.
No child-labor involved.
Bite me, bite me, bite me.
The End of Daydreaming.
Show the fish the firewire.
When the whip comes down.
Of shamans and businessmen.
Even in the quietest moments.
Your light in a world of change.
Introducing Goofy Login Spoofer.
Show the digifish an empty ocean.
www... where the water can't flow.
Live as if you were to die tomorrow.
Put your money where your mouse is.
Too much candy gonna ride your soul.
Computers have a short life expectancy.
From black to gold and never back again.
Dotconnilingusto only goes a certain way.
Online unconsciousness as symbolic death.
The Grand Ragnarock 'n Funk Odyssey 2018.
Liposuction defines the American way of life.
The Silicon Chip Circus of Totalitarian Take-Over.
We're beyond the scope of Reason, you Droogies of e!
Armin Van Buuren is a waitress of the New Barbarism.
I don't speak Apple (and I don't speak Windows either).

½ of the world-population is connected, think about that.

When Information Technology became our drinking water.

Yer man Bono Christ and Pygmy beliefs concerning public psychosis.

77% of children in the capital city of Bangladesh, Dhaka, are watching porn.

Earth, fire, 7UP, giga-bite, Pepsi Light and pathological meditation on bones.

With spite.

Buy now again.

Long, long, long.

Sign Up For Life.

Squeeze the fruit.

Here we go again.

Create Ad Libitum.

1 Reader Comment.

Middle of Nowhere.

Fridays I'm In Love.

Them Heavy People.

The weakness in me.

Ape Escape Academy.

Lost on some horizon.

You burnt all my cd's!

Don't do what you do!

Jazz, and all that funk.

Having a conversation.

My eyes are falling out.

Things I miss the most.

Popular in your network.

Pay your bills from anywhere.

Portable storage for the paranoid.

My cyber-optic breakfast, everyday.

This is the hardest story I've ever told.

Prehistoric Pop-Art for a New America.

iRoadmovie + Redux Deluxe (that's all fine!).

Look and sound like a rockstar straight away.

Mummy, when you'll be a boy, you'll have a willy!

Welcome to the BBQ King Habsburger Steakhouse!

Web-surfing and developmental coordination disorder.

Become hunter or hunted in a world of unrelenting horror.

Don't waste your life Claire, don't waste your busfare Claire.

More than 3 billion minds aligned at the same moment in time.

Somewhere between psychedelics and an astute business instinct.

The shells I find on the beach tell me one day the world will be as one.

Comandante Mike Cobbs ft. Subcomandante Flea: The Powers of Equality.

Bison habitat destruction and biomedical diagnosis and treatment of depression.

Little bit of love... little bit of love, little bit of love, little bit of love, little bit of love...

Rewriting Warhol: Campbell Soupcomandante Bootsy Collins a 1000 times in diamond dust.

The Big Molokomodo: Where Is The What If The What Is In Why? (Live At Java Jazz Festival).

Go fund me.

Death denied.

Royal with Cleese.

You had me at hello.

I lost my memory card.

Stupid is as stupid does.

Technology is a queer thing.

Starbucks and vampire bats.

10 Funniest Celebrity Deaths.

There's someone else I got to be.

I feel the need – the need for speed.

The appDonald's Big MacBook of Jobs.

Modern technology owes ecology an apology.

The Night of the Long Teeth (I'm The Walrus).

(A friend) Like Ben (Like Ben) Like Uncle Ben's.

Jim Jarmusch, Turtle First Aid, Independence Day.

The Diamondback Terrapin Turtle Geezer, c'est moi!

Gold digging inside Joseph Campbell's Soup Bubbles.

No machine can do the work of one extraordinary man.

David Beckham Instinct Aftershave for Homo rhodesiensis.

Uncle Ben Harper's Black Rice To Power (Get Up Stand Up!).

Turtle Rescue, Turtle Adoption and In-Group / Out-Group therapy.

Autostop, Miss Dooda, Gordon Cooper, Pin-Up Girl, Space Guardians.

Paleo-Indian Peacock Soft shelled turtles bathing in the Memory Motel online.

The genocide of Brazil's indigenous people and 29 of the best Neymar hairstyles.

Jackie Kennedy: The Black Widow and her Tomato Trillion Dollar Beef Noodles.

ChaOS X.

iKilotunes.

Lying eyes.

Purchased.

Cracking up.

Fish 'n chips.

Sweet dreams?

Parallel worlds.

Stocks to watch.

e-Mails can wait.

Billerickie Dickie.

Stock to exchange.

Wars and charities.

It's all ultimate stuff!

World of Uncertainty.

www... the nightmare.

Reptiles and anonimity.

Scanning my limitations.

Hardware Pour Hommes.

Every cashflow has its ebb.

A fireplace... nothing like it.

Between web and rock art sites.

The millennium jump of Capital.

Call of Cthulhu: The Wasted Land.

Speedway (Theme from Fastlane).

Surviving High School in America.

You're my favourite business model!

Prozac, e-masonry and night terrors.

Because the night belongs to hackers.

The fifth member of the nuclear family.

I know a composer who prefers the piano.

Tristan did not meet Isolde on the internet.

A book resting on your belly... how peaceful!

To facilitate e-banking, tell us your life story.

Virtual scuba diving does not help schizophrenics.

We don't have anything you need in stock right now!

You look like a f* crocodile leather iPhone case-study!

Spirituality by means of technology gives no meaning.

10 Programming languages you should learn right now.

Wireless communications... the Native Indians were good at it.

Open Source wellness, celebrity perfumes and spirit language disorder.

Lady Gaga's Fame Black Fluid Eau de Parfum and fire-origin from vagina.

Fibergate.

No backup.

Hyperfighter.

Accept the lie.

You can see me.

You say Dubai...

North Sea Funk.

Dutch Internet Mountain.

Some boys couscous and don't Intel.

Create as many questions as you like.

The Native Indian Flint Festival of Tools.

Don't panic, your files are safely backed up!

Florida Here We Come: Betty & Jebby Boob!

McHorny Highness Bill Clinton doesn't inhale.

Jeb Bush is an all American boy, yes, a sex-symbol.

Donald, what do you actually do for a living in fact?

Personally inducting Madonna in the Hall of Shame.

The Complete Microsoft Mon Amour Catalogue Raisonné.

Apple Certified Brillo Soaps pads used in digital, ritual washing.

Stone arrowheads, bone arrow points and force quit applications.

Adolf Wölfli's Campbell's Tabasco Soup, now in Stone Age America.

Collecting whalebones for the sake of collecting whalebones, what else?

Native American artefacts and kitsch diamond-encrusted buffalo skulls.

Rewriting Warhol: 32 Camay's Tomato Soap Cans 1 time in mellow yellow.

The Computer World's reduction of Language to a pornographic minimum.

These massive seagulls picked my eyes out halfway on the Internet Mountain.

Dale Mac Cooper, Anti-Theft Backup group 1, Kellogg's Stone Flakes and blades.

Bill Gates' search for common ground between God and technological evolution.

'I'll box that Dutch sicko around the block if he dares to take his pants off.' Donald Trump.

Frank Zappa's Baby Snakes, Internet Mountain Goat Skulls and Apple Certified Beyoncé lyrics.

Creep.

The Curse.

Out of print.

Tap to install.

Inbetweenies.

USAvida Dollars.

The Bumpy Ride.

The Gates of Hell.

Survive if you can.

Spotify Your Acne.

Dark Fall: Lost Souls.

Baby, You're A Rich Man!

Ohh des scrabouchinanas!

Ping a contact, pong a friend.

Disconnected from the heart.

You are what you are watching.

Van Gogh saw Virtuality coming.

Inside Out: Kubistarickabraquerelle!

Ian Dury: Sweet Gene Vincent Van Gogh.

Upside down: Online Baselitzkriegsszapp!

In The White Steakhouse, Washington DC.

Digital pregnancy leads to virtual caesarians.

The Internet Mountain Gorilla (Self-Portrait.

Non-Orphic elements attributed to Steve Jobs.

What is called 'bird's milk' is the white of the ego.

Just ZAPP between these lines, you Droogies of e!

News, celebrities, celeb news, celebrity gossip, disaster news.

High on the fascism-scale once more over and over and over...

Shooting balloons with Todd Rundgren (Gratis in Bobbejaanland!).

'Microsoft Mon Amour is Tim Cook's psychedelic breakfast.' Ziggy Pops.

Wrecking The Middle-East... a Neo-Condolézard Riceye-Popping Bushes job.

Comandante Che Chuevara ft. Marshall J. Hendrix: All Along The Watchtower P1.

Bigfoot Mac.

World Total.

The Evil iMac.

All About Apes.

Terms of Service.

The Cloud of Inner Speech.

What's App, Dr. Funkenstein?

Warner Brothers picked them up...

Bison corpses rotting on American soil.

Don't triple your double luck the first time!

Virtual missiles to defend a warped Humanity.

Big MacBook Pro-Life: A Republican preference.

A machine would choose to be a machine if it could.

Watching the wolves chasing you across America Online.

Far and wide, once upon a time: stones, steppes and savannas.

Bison population crash and its effect on the indigenous people.

Why public companies have a big disadvantage with hot startups.

Me, MyGlass, myself, & I No (Yes!) New Holland Lady Corry DADA.

Uncle Sim, Uncle Tim, Uncle Sam, Uncle Tom, Major Tom, John Major.

My bowels bleeding with Artpop-gigabytes in a post-Hirst, amphibian afterworld.

Wendy Williams & The BBQ Wendy Whopper Singers: (Do the) Long Island Chicken.

The Modern American Bison Murder Squad Bandstand exploding the veins of Capital.

Walk On By.

Personal cash.

Buy something!

Insects are interactive.

Baby you're a cyberstar!

Mammoths and bankers.

A mouse is one-hand job.

What's On A Man's Disc?

The best cyclone of my life.

Hired, wired, fired, shot, dead.

Prelude to the end of the game.

Peak performances all day long.

Lord of the Heavenly Web Hosts.

The day your mouse became a rat.

(We'll be) Hangin' on The Telephone.

Paleo Earth, Psycho Globe, Pop Planet.

You do have a common Client Interface.

The driving force behind hybrid warfare.

The Kalimantan Chainsaw Massacre 1997.

Video games are the toys of mass destruction.

Down by The Highway we sat down and wept.

Swimming online you are bound to meet sharks.

Who is the Versace of the pharmaceutic industry?

Up-to-date and out-of-order live in the same street.

Population, World Population, Real World Population.

I am he as you are he as you and we are all in this together.

Dress Your Bump: 11 Inspiring Maternity Dresses That Are Fit For a Queen.

James Black, BlackBerry White ft. Purple Hayes: Chocolate Salty Balls Live.

Most of our moves are the virtual reconstruction of the earliest Paleo-Indian bison trail.

My Saves.

Megadeal.

We're sorry.

No surprises.

The PC Police.

Done too soon.

Mean Machine.

Recommended.

God, guns, g-spit.

Creating illnesses.

See all you can see.

Fifty shades of filth.

And down we went.

Orange Mécanique.

Live Nation is dead!

No news, good news.

LinkedIn like a shot fox.

Nature hitting America!

Foreskin, eel-fat, MacAir.

Net-threats by e-cowards.

Will they ever give us a break?

The Blizzard of US, the people.

We advise you to buy a new one.

Pop-up help always comes too late.

The Elvis of the Digital Revolution.

Digital Abstinence is what is called for.

Betel chewing among the Yahoo Tribes.

Flag a problem (Stars, Bones & Stripes).

You Are Not Connected To The Internet.

Into The Cruyff (RIP Johan Groove Edit).

Print that hamburger while it is still alive!

World Wars: The Yahoos versus the Googles.

Kentucky Fraud Chicken comin' home to roost.

+ Follow, Search Web, Now Watching, Up Next.

The Black Bass Dictator: Linley Marthe My Dear.

Before They Pass Away (The Rolling Stones World-Tour 2018).

I know some autumn leaves which don't want to leave the world.

Tribal Tiffany-twisted elegance for the American middle-classes.

I majored in Computer Science but hate the career opportunities.

Sergeant Klark Kent: I Don't Care If You Really Want To Put Me Down.

A sanctuary offering a variety of dining facilities complimented by Chiquita bananas.

Yahoo Politics: your daily Yahoo stories for Afterlife, World Perfect and Purgatory visits.

Continue.

Space Noir.

Dignity lost.

Cloning kills.

Free delivery.

Into The Void.

Different world.

Washington PC.

California Speed.

Artificial Stupidity.

Mozart was human.

Jeff Buckley: Grace.

Pencils and rubbers.

Phone didn't charge?

The Fable of the Bites.

This Is What We Find.

The Clash: The Call-Up.

What makes a good life?

Change is a mere second.

Ring Ring It's seven A.M.

We want our bisons back!

Our poor, bleeding hearts.

Slash 'n Burn, I'm watching.

For the greater good of God.

(Don't) do anything you want.

Chicken Frenzy: Director's Cut.

You gotta walk it like you talk it.

We simplify it especially for YOU!

Gods, giants and graphic designers.

And the Oscar goes to... Kokoschka!

Terminator 3: Rise Of The Machine.

Yes, I did sleep with Oprah Winfrey.

Don't get locked out of your account.

Download the Burger King App here.

F*! My MacBook Pro is still working!

First Class internet, second class wifi.

1.400 bananas, 76 towns & 1 million people.

I'm a looser baby (so why don't you kill me?).

Is this the 1980s, or is my mind playing tricks?

Shop online, visit a store, call Apple, and pay up.

Cow wallpaper, quasi-pornography and Diet Coke.

Web Techniques (23 positions in a one night stand).

Lots of friends in cyberspace but lonely on the Earth.

Gimme Honda, Gimme Sony, so cheap and real phony.

The price of concert tickets really has become an issue.

Nothing beats a coffee and a newspaper in the morning.

Bison priscus, MacBook Pro, Basquiat, Vogue Magazine.

From the weakness of our senses we cannot judge the truth.

Steve Jobs schools and developmental coordination disorder.

Big Paul MacCarthy's Santa Kloss' Gibbon now in Disneyland.

David Beckham Classic Deodorant for Homuncules patagonicus.

The old glaucoma doesn't help looking through the Apple Glasses.

Hong Kong dollars and Indian cents, English pounds and Eskimo pence.

Rewriting Warhol: Campbell's Super Monkey Ballroom Tomato Blitzoup.

Dr. Dre urBeats, 'me-too'-sufferers and bison funk surveillance of the world.

Brings you back to this awful place, knuckle merchants and you bankers, too.

Bamako Express: Samba Touré, Anansy Cissé & Black Mango Big Band: Crocodile Blues.

Givers of Courage: Thousand of wild American bison appear from nowhere at Standing Rock.

Decline.

myMusic.

How to sell.

Search or enter.

Where are you?!

Share Happiness.

Take a quick tour.

Snakes and cables.

We have forgotten.

The Divided Selfie.

Join Other Network.

I want to be just here!

Yelp! I need somebody!

Trois Saisons En Enfer.

Easy drivers, raging balls.

Having this, we want that.

Living in the Age of Smart.

Hey... What Planet Is This?

A little dab'll do ya Donald!

Apocalypse: Trending Now.

I feel terribly tagged myself.

What is computer language?

Thinking outside the chat-box.

Change is the erosion of memory.

African Freedom (Made in China).

Not to know which page you're on.

Insomnia, insomnia, everywhere...

Native American Knife Sheath $ 24,00.

Welcome pueblos indígenas de México!

Poverty rates and multinational generosity.

Stupidity is fashionable at this moment in time.

Ordering French fries from the MacBook Menu.

The extreme-right on the virtual rise everywhere.

Where the poor can think they will be rich one day.

Microsoft Mon Amour: The Book You Take To War.

Je ne trouve pas mon téléphone débile, mon amour.

Delete files, foul lies, loose ends and drippery details.

The definition of a real path is you can't walk it again.

Exclusive Tailoring for Proper Fit to Support a Man's Needs.

Birds, beauty, Bushmen, Buy Now, Buy Here, Bigfoot, Black Elk.

Apple users, beer-drinkers, hell-raisers and darknet-marketeers.

Brilliant tweet by Kanye West on Xenophanes' concept of God today.

Acne Warhol, G-Spotify, Cookie-O-Puss, teenage nightmare, Taylor Swift.

Techno is rhythm for machine men with machine minds and machine hearts.

You lot! What? Don't stop Give it all you got – You lot! What? Don't stop Yeah!

Pause.

Black Hole.

Shop by brand.

What time is it?

Save your favourite.

Turning the webpage.

The Internet Explodes.

I have 10.000 Hate Me's!

Le Paradis – un peu plus loin.

Boyzone are the Irish Beatles.

AirDrop the bomb on Facefuck.

Magic, religion and the Internet.

Who am I, and if not here, where?

Your weekly mixtape of fresh music.

Thank Our Finger-Lickin' Good God 2!

The Efficient Casino of Conspiracy Theory.

You always find me in the kitchen at parties.

Steve Jobs, sharks and zoogony of Anaximander.

The Great MacDonald Trumpadelic Gop 'n Roll Swindle.

The Schizo Nile Aristocrat Brigade returns to the land of e.

Celebrity perfumes in the US and Paleo-Indian product reviews.

Silicon breasts, lipo-sucked derrières and Ronald MacDonald's clowns.

Jon Bono Jovi & KKK Lynrd Skynrd All-Stars: Schwanz Home Alabama.

Name!

Lord o.

REJECT!

AutoLISP.

Prinz Horn.

The Scream.

Shop by type.

All Greek to me.

Young and Rich.

Discover Weekly.

White Man Is Dead.

Dream a little dream.

Take The Tour Merch.

Mourning in America.

Attitude is everything.

Hot of the press no more.

The Powersockets of Myth.

I hope Carl Jung will remember.

See what your friends are playing.

Rotary phones are not for squares.

Let Me Watch ft. Apani B. as Nikki.

Gerber son wifi fait mal à personne.

The David Beckham Signature Story.

Podcasts, Audiobooks, Spoken World.

Adele 19, 21, 25, 39, 54, 69, 89, 103, 119, 157.

For we all came forth from earth and water.

Hollywood buddhism and Capri-Battery acid.

Life in the fast lane (The Information Highway).

Happiness does not reside in Google or Chrome.

Where there's a machine, death is never far away.

Not that easy to write a book about anything at all.

The Great Slaughter of the American Bison Herds.

AXIOMERICA: Material ft. Shabbat Ranks | Reality.

Now, What Do You Want From Live, Remote Control.

A bunch of binge-eating braggers, that's all there's to it.

Next – Shopping in Nigeria: An amazon.com for Africa?

Uncle Ben Carson's Country Inn Rice (#BeginWithBen).

Tes phrases oubliées se retrouvent dans ma rivière perdue.

The American dream is a burning, constant, sense of bulimia.

Bits, atoms, bodies, coffins, after-life, Nespresso, Matt Damon.

National Lampoon, Mondo Bondage, tech control and tv-dinners.

Please read this software licence carefully before you kick the bucket tomorrow.

Bison Bush Doctors, Campbell's McDonald Duck Soup and American Psycho Killers.

Skip.

Bad hombres.

Speed demon.

Out of Stream.

Free I.T. for life.

You speak LISP?

Push the envelop!

The Disconnected.

Sir Paleo Pepsi Pop.

Bigger than Bigfoot?

Jay Z Christ Superstar.

Contact Our Help Desk.

Madness to the Method.

Controlling the e-Storm.

If iPhone 6 were iPhone 9.

U got the power, now use it!

We make life easier for YOU!

Continuity What Continuity?

Pull all plugs everywhere, now!

Funkhansa Crashteam Reunion.

I Want You Too! Be Made Clean!

Bono Christ is genuinely humble.

Microsoft: Natural, fresh & ready.

Sarah Palin: Mounting the Python.

Yahoo Originals and Google Fakes.

Tricks, toads, tours, tickets, turtles.

It's the mouse that moves the hand.

Snakes. Why'd it have to be snakes?

Restrain your consumption of media.

Thirty Seconds To Mars: This Is War!

The appDonald's Big MacBook of Jobs.
Fat, fatigue and online spirit possession.
Among Machines we shall dance and die.
High Tech Hoovers for hulky handsomes.
Seems like the world knows nothing at all.
We went to America to make some money.
Modern technology owes ecology an apology.
Nature on display in soap commercials online.
The Pros & Cons of Searching Your Date Online.
Buying realtime crackers to feed elephants online.
Toto, I have a feeling we're not in Kansas anymore.
Jim Jarmusch, Turtle First Aid, Independence Day.
Celebrity masks and other camouflage self-portraits.
The effect of Online Palaeontology on the teenage brain.
Elvis Presley, psychoactive eagle and origins of shamans.
The last thing this country needs is another Bush, indeed.
Utopian orderings at the psychiatric facility nearest to you.
As far as I'm concerned, progress peaked with frozen pizza.
Billy 'Jean' Gates (like a beauty queen from a movie scene).
We went to America to impose freedom on the Red Nation...
Major Tim Cookle, narcissistic personality and the Rainbow.
John Curry Heinz Tomato Ketchup XBox-lunch at the Y-river.
BIFF, Wrecking Ball, NRA Rhythm Nation, Jay ZZ Top Over The Pops.
Video games, homocide rates and unspecified Underworld whirlwinds.
It is appallingly obvious that our technology has exceeded our humanity again.
Paleo-Indian Peacock Soft shelled turtles bathing in the Memory Motel online.
Digital wallpaper, American Sidekick turtles and Dinosaur gun violence statistics.
Rewriting Warhol: Menstrual taboos in Mezosoic North America 11 times in orange.
Sauvage, Johnny Depp, mud turtles, fleshly pleasures and the mediocrity of the occult.
Obey!
Get now.
Stairway to Hell.
Kingdom of liars.
Push my buttons.
Eyes are precious.
Become a partner.
Blocky Kind of Love.
Fiber is not working.
In A Changing Society.

About Vodafone Nigeria.

Google gagging the world.

PC, solarium, discothèque.

BlackBerry White of course.

Sexual Life in Ancient China.

Everything's coming our way.

And other specified deliriums.

A Monster Ate My Homework.

I want you too 2 pay your taxes.

World, spirit world, Cyberspace.

The rotten Apple spoils the barrel.

Nothing mostly happens every day.

Building poor-to-poor applications.

With mixed anxiety and depressed mood.

Just call and talk to an astrologer directly.

The idea of a lifetime, everyday, soon, now.

Help, about, mobile, people, cookies, developers.

Nothing is said in a cybercafé, let alone discussed.

Chipping, Fripping, tripping, stripping and drilling.

Rewriting Warhol: Marylin Manson 11 times in silver.

Asking dangerous questions you get dangerous answers.

Yoga, hosting, jogging, chilling, meditating, working out.

Nowhere Man, Pocket Adventures, Samsung Galaxy Life.

Virtual Insanity, Brat Pitt's testicles and the God particle.

Rewriting Warhol: The Velvet Underground Coca-Cola Zero.

Sarah Palin & Red Hat Linux Peppers: Mad Hatter's Tea Party Club Mix.

All you want.

Recharge online.

Let There Be Byte!

The Thinking Object.

Gods versus humans.

Atomic Bomber Man.

That's gonna cost you...

D'Angelo for President!

Pop is an orgy of names.

Your mother should know.

Don't you start bugging me.

Defining the Idiom of Funk.

The Naked Whipclip Launch.

New Snowden, Old Snowden.

Legal uploads, illegal downloads.

Without any installation hassles?

Eradication of Riches is the real challenge.

Kilobytes, megabytes, gigabytes, metabytes.

Viktor & Rolf Posh Spicebomb Eau de Toilet.

Byte, botox, butter, beavers, bottoms, beta blockers.

James White & The Contortions: Sensation White.

Open Source Mediocrity, Stone Age Schizophrenia.

What a waste of time, energy, electricity, eccentricity.

Amsterdam is the Stutterheimat of the New Barbarism.

I Funk Therefore I Am (Never Mind The Ku Klux Klan).

IBM's Deep Blue-crowned motmot (Momotus Momota).

Remember, no matter where you go online, there you are.

This day in History: Anniversary of the Ice Cream Sundae.

Cyber aphasia, animal otherness, Christian slave morality.

Internet, melancholia and the paleo psychoanalysis of dreams.

Names, trademarks, logos, designs, text, graphics and other bullshit.

MacArthur Park, porn again Christians and White Lord Creator Disorder.

The obvious practical advantages aside, the Internet remains a terrible meal.

Dysphoric and elevated mood, pre-lithic pipe smoking and the Brides of Funkenstein.

Hell No!

Jammed.

I'm cryin'.

Just pull it.

Dance away.

Phantom Dust.

Contort yourself.

The sadness of it all.

Hosting and jogging.

Meet the new Y-Box.

The Doomstrump Thinkers.

Stray Cats: Stray Cat Strump.

Chaos League: Sudden Death.

Laptops, lungfish and lemurs.

Kids don't answer cell phones.

No Drum Can Take This Blow!

You can't win a computergame.

Jump over your shadow people.

Whalebones and motherboards.

Where there is bite there is death.

You're a driver not a passenger in life.

Sixty Seconds To Venus: This Is Love!

Virtuality, psychosis and human nature.

You need to upgrade your life right now!

Ninety Seconds To Jupiter: This Is Funk!

Laughter to those who strive for long life.

CBS This Morning: The Bush Perspective.

They are people who want EVERYTHING.

Into the blue again, after the money's gone.

USAMERICANA: Material | The Third Power.

TV-biscuits, radio-gateaux and PC-patisseries.

Donald Fagen for Secretary of Keyboard Affairs.

Dolphins caressing your softest skin, mon amour.

Breaking the barriers between music and technology.

Never Known Questions: 5 decades of The Residents.

Sony, Samsung and Paleo-oriental prototype disorders.

Do we really want to hurt ourselves, do we really want to make ourselves cry?

Girly Gates: 1 l. vodka, 4 oz. orange juice, 2 oz. Buloxyethanol, phosphoric acid salt.

The Rise and Fall of the Modern Machine in our lives, yesterday today and tomorrow.

Rewriting Warhol: Yes, we have no bananas today today (Costa Rica Banana Radio Edit).

Calvin Klein's hypersexual new ad campaign is creeping people out, just like in the old days.

re:Pent.

Go ad-free!

Dead souls.

HiGH LiFE.

Save Money.

In difference.

Data and Life.

Can't find this.

Stars Are Blind.

Lobsters in love.

A matter of time.

Radarhead I Am.

Apple Bloody Apple.

The SNOBOL Effect.

Can I borrow a fiver?

The pyramid of myth.

Like... like... like ME!

Of Brillo and baboons.

Digits, drums, dreams.

Rachid Taha: Ya Raya...

I heard the mission bell.

Bring all to the frontline!

Macaques and MacBooks.

Vamos A La Playa Ivanka!

Underclocking wintertime.

We don't need the firewater.

Télécharge your intravision.

Yesterday you said tomorrow.

Tagged, lost and downgraded.

Indios mexicanos, Hallelujah!

Pleasing people the world over.

Bill Laswell: The western lands.

I'm a natural man down all I can...

That I am suffocating in this world.

Things to watch as you trade today.

Watch what your friends are seeing.

Silver Scar Crash (Double Disaster).

Fela Kuti: Beasts of No Great Nation.

The Cabbage Difference Engine Nr. 2.

Know your phone before it knows you.

Tu ne reçois pas mes sms, mon amour?

Flippy patients with floppy complaints.

Let's go, let's go for a ride in the country.

A mental beach for an hallucinated ocean.

Rambo, Rimbaud, Reason, Reincarnation.

The face of the BBC: Jim 'Criminal' Saville.

Sticking my hydrocephalic head into my PC.

Mind Over Matter: The images of Pink Floyd.

Remove the water at the bottom of the ocean!

You won't find the ol' Gilgamusk on Linkedin.

It's not what you wear – it's what's in your heart.

AXIOMERICA: Axiom Funk | Funkcronomicon.

The Miracle of Joey Ramone (Tim Cook Club Mix).

Bow Wow Wow: The Man Internet Mountain 1983.

The ritual vomiting of the worldwideweb's remains.

I am very sad and desperate, my body hurts all over.

OneRepublican Presidential Race: We'll be counting stars.

Red Bill Clinton: 2 cans Red Bull, White Martini Dry, gasoline.

Britney Spears Fantasy eau de perfume and bison livers bleeding.

USAXIOMERICA: Simon Shaheen | The Music of Mohamed Abdel Wahab.

The word 'Funky' comes from the Congolese 'Lu Fuki', meaning 'Creative Sweat'.

Strawberry Spangled Banner: 1 l. Martini Rosato, 4 l. strawberry juice, Downfrost HD Fluid.

Digibesitas.

Tiny hands.

Knowbocop.

I bet you like it.

Both ends burn.

Happy together.

Man, Mail, Magic.

Tourette? Click here.

Dare to be indifferent.

Toy boys and cell girls.

O it fell out upon a day.

I screenshot my manager.

Beyond RAM and Reason.

Software to keep off ghosts.

Who says humans can't buy?

We are in the middle of a swell.

Networking equals social aerobics.

Futures made of vermicular reality.

Jestofunk: Find Your State Of Mind.

Never lost a novel without a back-up?

You only want me for my virtual body!

Decoding the propaganda of profitability.

Printer Control Language can be abusive.

We share a collective memory and it's free.

Activism is what we call Irish pornography.

Protestants like SMS, catholics love chatting.

Old World Technology, New World Sexuality.

A journey into the Net knows no homecoming.

The iMacCarthy list, you're on it too you know!

Offline masochists morphing into online sadists.

In electronic Nature, the hunted don't know fear.

Where whales still understand each other... the sea...

The heart is the gateway to the Unseen World, to the Spirit World.

The hands of children are making the tools of adults as you are reading.

Pulptastic e-commerce, chicken fat and Paleo Power Point representations.

The white people never wanted to learn before. They thought we were savages.

Mr. Joe Bowie & 3rd Defunkt Anti-Funk Army Division: Thermonuclear Sweat.

'That guy Bob Laswell is importing terrorist music inside our borders folks, yes, terrorist tunes.'

Rewriting Warhol: Stevie Nicks & The Blue Velvet Underground (Dole Class Premium Bananas).

Hide.

Do to me.

Fill the gap.

What now?!

Born into IT.

More to come.

Save your soul!

American Spirit.

The Discourse of i.

A long and happy life.

Of iBooks and impalas.

What's with the Chinaman?

White powder, black market.

Banging the bricks of Reason.

Neil Jung: Waging Heavy Peace.

Command and Conquer: Red Alert.

The outline of one's inner life-story.

Spiritual teachings and business finance.

Tattooed soccer-players ain't no warriors.

The Apple Genius Bar... here I come again!

The computer wasn't invented on a computer.

Carlos Chaplin + Santana Big Band: Tribute to Prince.

You can not get to the library of Ashurbanipal by mouse.

AXIOMERICA: Henry Threadgill | Too Much Sugar For A Dime.

The creator designed the human being to cry. Crying is a release.

Starry night, campfire light, and the coyote calls where the howlin' winds will.

Flash in the pan.

New ways to connect.

Scuba-diving into byte.

Work with us or perish.

Only geeks can be geeks.

Bison tails and dating sites.

Loona Tune: Vamos A La Playa!

Kickstarting The Bison Funk Army.

View Life as analog and death as digital.

Demons, techno music and video games.

Talking Heads: Burnin' Down The House!

Haitian voodoo can bring down the internet.

Watch the Apple Watch the Apple Watch film.

System Preferences: Spotlight on Otis Redding.

Living a life of constant change and make-overs.

Donald Trump: The Rocky Horror Picture Show.

Tribal World Wars: The Facebooks vs The Apples.

Paranoia, surveillance, Starbucks Coffee, bison habitat resurrection.

The Brothers Johnson & Johnson: Skin I'm In (Skin & Hair Care Club Remix).

Loving-kindness, Monica Lewinsky and Uncle Jeb's White Rice House aspirations.

Bill Laswell ft. Eraldo Bernocchi & 7 Tibetan Monks (Kalimpong Monastery): Mun Pa.

Ring my bell.

Try Jah Love.

No sympathy.

Bird on the wire.

So much trouble.

Make a statement.

Space Invaders 1978.

The Nature of Money.

It ain't over till it's over.

Leave Page, leave World.

Mania, Crisis, depression.

Memory gone, memory lost.

What it is to be human, online.

And you may ask yourself: how do I work this?

See me burning.

Macworld War 3.

Pick up the pieces.

The Digital Family.

Exporting anorexia.

Yahooligans all over.

Too much information.

Films are better friends.

Don't let Daddy kiss me.

Every PC knows its grave.

Confessions in a chat box.

The Memory of the World.

Still crashing the same PC.

How many mazes in a Net?

Email doesn't even ring once.

Online you never wank alone.

Digital dreams are programmed.

The Internet deserves a meteorite.

A real Amazon only has one breast.

Jeb Koons' Artpop for Gaga Glitter.

The Cubist Comet, New York, 2689.

Microsoft's Definite Guide to Fascism.

Reading the clouds one know as much.

AWB: There's always someone waiting.

Great Spirit, teach me to be a heart warrior.

In the beginning there was Microsoft Word.

Roll me over and turn me around. Let me keep spinning till I hit the ground.

And we're Jebbin' in the name of the Lord... (Bush Ambient Miami Beach Dub).

Little Donny Osmond: Long-Haired Lover From Liverpool (Trump Club Remix).

'I will sue the Mexican rapist from Holland through his commie ass, yes I will.' D. Trump.

21 Instagrams.

Open Your Heart.

Difesa della Natura.

Remember tomorrow.

Connected to the teeth.

Dream To The Rhythm.

Have A Little Faith In Me.

There's wifi in the cosmos.

Paul Breitner was in Tavares.

I heard the news today oh boy.

The stones from my enemies...

The Google Chromosome Disasters.

Delete everything, remember nothing.

Red Hot Pino Peppers: Stadium Palladino.

Dream On Dreamer – Life is in your hands.

Prehistoric and native hunting was beautiful.

We shall cross that bridge when we come to it.

Digital rain-charms and American Psycho Therapy.

White Collar Dreamtime has come to the earth and it riches.

Gilbert & George's Grandmaster Flash Gordon's Gin Sculpture.

Julius Bär | Your Wealth Manager | Discover our visionary approach.

Humanity Astray: We can't even slaughter our own pineapples anymore.

Thin Lizzy Taylor & Johnny Guitar Walker's Dance Heroes: Whiskey In The Jar.

iTunes Mega Store, online bison surveillance and cookery programming language.

The Platters: Jebb Tide (At last we're face to face and as we kiss through an embrace).

'Stronger than dirt. Dirtier than Donald Duck, Goofy and Ice Age 3 together.' Newsweek.

He who swallows 'udala' (apple) seed must consider the size of his anus. ~ African proverb.

Guns, Roses and Johnny Walker's November Rain-making among Republican grass rooters.

Say no!

Bosch Urus.

School's Out!

Pressure drop.

Never Say Die!

H of Mammals.

Come as you are.

Too hot to handle.

Run with the pack.

Houses of the Holy.

Bison versus robots.

The Best of Spinners.

10cc: Deceptive Bends.

Betty Wright: Hard To Stop.

The Tubes: Young And Rich.

www.quickanddirtytips.com.

I want my robot to be a blonde.

Do good in the face of Broadband.

Aztec robots will still vote Pacific.

Where the buffaloes were abundant.

A waste of space and a waste of time.

Microchips are the dandruff of the dollar.

Distribution and origin of Life in America.

Noam Chomsky's America – Eau de Toilet.

Rewriting Warhol: Fossil Bison Wallpaper.

Why don't your answer my mails straightaway?!

Hey man... the Apocalypse... it's happening man, cool!

Seven valid species of fossil bison have been recognized.

They ate our food, and forgot our names. ~ Tunisian Proverb.

Waltzing my robot into the dusty sunset of Britpop Oblivion.

Our robots' genitals won't give way to a barbarian sexuality, or...?
The influence of the Buffalo environment upon Indian mentality.
The Parkerilla, Red River Settlement and Yes, Going For The One.
Sugar Hilarius Ganges: Rapper's Delight (Bombay Gin Radio Edit).
Sleep.
Get Info.
Now bed.
Be damned.
Fun Anyone?
Balls Of Steel.
Working 34/7.
I ate the bones.
I said Not Now.
Getting started.
HipHop On Ice.
The Royal Scam.
Steamy Windows.
I'm Lovin' What?!
PCWORLD's End.
The Viral Sermon.
Force quit Reason.
Persona Non Grata.
Enters the Interpols.
Safety first, funk later.
(We're in a) Heatwave.
Because you're worth it.
Money back guaranteed.
Hope, change, desillusion.
Les Magiciens De La Soul.
Failed to open your mouth.
Redeem, Account, Support.
The Smarter Way To Suffer.
Inside Lionel Richie's mind.
You can't buy me love online.
In praise of the American Eagle.
Watching the detectives Part 22.
Mammoth, what's a Funkadelic?
Me, myself & IBM Informix-4GL.
Introducing The Pink Panther Party.

Tu est ma muse parce que tu m'amuse.

This day in History, and any other day.

He has always been a bit selfie that guy.

Spell Checker: Language Not Sustained.

We're seriously running out of FaceTime.

Another family crisis: the robot goes blind.

A robot's cry may be wilder but it has no soul.

On the web, the river of Life swells with tears.

The Hillary McClinton Double Dogg Pounder.

The Paris Hilton Hotel California Wet Dream.

Blue turtles don't listen to Sting in general but I do.

Uncle Ben's Black Rice To Power: Funk It What It Is.

A privacy reminder from Google... I get one every day.

The Austrian Empire Ronald McAdolf Trump Burger.

AXIOMERICA: Ronal Shanon Jackson | Red Warrior.

Bill Gates, Micky Melissa and Pueblo tribal birds forms.

Geographic Sound Archaeology: Ahmed Fakroun 'Nisyan' 2016.

George, Bush & The Bison Funk All-Stars: One Nation Under A Hoof.

Shop by price.

Print your life.

Get your fight on.

Fear of Facebook.

I'm walking a line.

Worm in my brain.

Napoleon: Total War.

iDSM-5 available now.

It just may be a one-shot deal.

Disk-drive for mental cripples.

Zoom in zoom out come the freaks...

Remote control is essentially female.

This computer has left to meet its maker!

Once in a lifetime, water flowing underground.

Comandante Kim Clarke: Female Bass Tornado.

Kurt Wagner's Götterdammerung Live from Nashville.

Werner Herzog's L'eau and behold: The human side of the digital revolution.

Britney Spears Circus Fantasy Eau de Toilet, celestial descent and soul recovery.

Wait For Sugar Hillary Clinton & The Brides of Funk-Them-Another-Mother Further!

Down by the rivertual insanity we sat down and whipped (It's a crazy world we're living in).

Fast baby.

Dirty work.

Take it easy.

Easy does it.

Get my 10% off.

Crazy like them.

Get special deals.

Walk the rockway.

B-box ain't Bebop.

Connection failure.

Bob Dylan: SAVED.

Sleep with the dark.

Force quit the world.

Gamers Anonymous.

Yes, we had iContact.

Never going back again.

Dancing in the Darknet.

Crash it crash it crash it.

Make Roma Great Again.

Game me where you can!

The Morning After Nature.

Behind the celebrity masks.

Till Microsoft does us apart.

All ends mean new beginnings.

Where on earth have you been?

Life is for sharing your privacy.

Rubio, Berlusconi's new toyboy.

A digital apocalypse means Life.

How to get rid of garden snakes?

Songs in the Function Key of Life.

Battlezone: Rise Of The Black Dogs.

Hungry hearts are for thirsty minds.

That printer got jammed once again.

My sleepers will flee to another America.

I lost my iPhone twice before it was stolen.

Avant-garde money and Google's Data Banks.

Giotto Dix & The Fauvist Orchestra: Photoshop.

Apple Product (RED) iPod nanobody's business.

Theologians and technicians serve the same cause.

Jebb Bush: Rolling with the tides (Spliff Dub Ambient).

Simple Subset Wizard and Dreambox Enigma Disasters.

There's no such thing as a digital evolution, it's an explosion.

A few hippies... a few nazis... that's how it all started in the Valley.

Trending Now: Captain America, Denver Broncos, Michael Moore, Dating sites.

A beautiful wall built by Mexican artists paid for by Bernie Sanders fans was the idea.

Run.

Try Now!

Need help?

Redirecting...

Already Gone.

God Damn I.T.!

Mon Mac et moi.

Open Happiness.

Ragnarok is here.

Get out of my life.

Access restricted.

Seen and not seen.

The Digital Divide.

Like me or hate me.

The Financial Tides.

I Learned It myWay.

Will they ever f* off?

Can't sleep anymore.

Fields of opportunity.

Dead men tell no tales.

Nietzsche: Jobs ist dead.

Faster than your shadow.

Gigabytes for the senseless.

Impossible are most things.

The damage is already done.

Synchronisant les attentants.

My psychiatrist, Ali Chemicali.

Systematic memory is never poetic.

Mean Girls: High School Showdown.

Delete your trust in the world HERE.

The Valley Bingo of the Shareholders.

Welcome to the Dotcomsumption Society.

Save me, save me, please come and save me.

Walking Down The Giant Frog Skull Avenue.

The world must be going somewhere or else...

Bruce Springsteen and Ali Farka Touré: The River.

The Destruction of the Information Technology Myth.

Firewalls, eating disorders and serpentine blood-lines.

The PPP Patas-Monkey I.T. Destruction Storm: Ape Is High.

Baby You're A Richman ft. The Modern Lovers: Egyptian Reggae.

Fossiles, dinosaur leg-bones and Internet World Penetration Rates.

The truth about hair extensions and globular white rhino horn rotation.

Hey man, back off, I'm your Eco kind of guy, I do good things in the world.

Trump Merch for Mexican rapists (Hello from the other side of the Apple screen!).

Walking the Red Road and thinking right is the greatest gift we can give to our children.

iClaudius.

Byte and day.

Cut The Crap.

Holland GAGA.

Live in America.

Hacking Habitat.

Never been lonier.

Bangladesh online.

Always On The Run.

The Coyote Dreaming.

Of bisons and bitcoins.

Loose yourself to dance.

Puking the Internet, daily.

Show me something beautiful.

Do you remember remembering?

War has no eyes. – Swahili saying.

Bernie: The First Hippie President.

I love yourselfie like I love myselfie.

Videogames and psychotic disorder.

What a beautiful world this could be.

Marco Rubio: A New American Century.

Lounge Beats by Jeb Bush – Deep and Trance.

My bowels ripped open by the Hyenas of Ownership.

There was a world without it, and there won't be another one.

We Want You for Prairie Prince Billy Bob's Bison Funk Army!

The Space Basement Jaxxigator Goonsquad: U Can't Stop Me.

Bugs, mudbugs, crawdads, yabbies, creekcrabs, chevaux de diable.

An army of sheep led by a lion can defeat an army of lions led by a sheep.

Ears that do not listen to advice accompany Bono's head when it is chopped off.

Sly Stone & The Family Stand: You Don't Have To Worry, Daddy Loves U So Much...

Destroy All.

Hacking Ikea.

Interneternitá!

Start Dictation.

I'm A Little Dinosaur.

Who do you think you are?

Bisons eat burgers nowadays.

Tut-Ankh-Amon... Hell Yeah!

www: The (2nd) Coming of Man.

Byte, risk, uncertainty and Paleo profit.

In search of the first programming language.

U2 Songs of Innocence Tattoo Shot €120,95.

The European Origins of American Thought.

Microsoft or the Anatomy of Industrial Order.

12 Terrifying Sea monsters no one can explain.

Password alternatives, Ice age crossings and pure wild bison.

I live on Long Island of the Pygmy Mammoth, what about you?

Do this before bed tonight to burn belly flab all night long (all night!).

Sly Stone & The Family Stand Circus Affair: Ghetto Heaven (12 Inch).

Apple Merch, Feel Classic Forgotten Fools and basic facts about bison.

Order Björn Borg's Classic Loungewear and DSM-5 Collection here and now!

Rewriting Warhol: Baxter Dury's Happy Campbell Soup Leaking At The Disco.

You're next!

Paper size matters.

Slow Brain Coming.

Apple: iFruitBomb 5.

Watching the detectives.

Random is as Random does.

Scams, sitcoms, schizophrenia.

Hot microchips and Waco Taco Sauce.

We were all once rain, we were all once lava.

Kendrick Lamar, the world's most famous raptor.

Is online pornography a problem for your business?

A world population giving way to electronic tyranny.

Bird Mimic schizophrenics and 100 recently extinct animals.

Visiting The Anti-Christiano Ronaldo MacDonaldo Trump Tower of Power.

Dotconsumption, Bulimia Nervosa, facial recognition and paleopsychopomp thunder.

iSniper 3D.

Gamed to kill.

MacBook Prodi.

Infinity Runner.

Silence is acceptance.

Zombie! Zombie! Zombie!

Clicking, clicking, clicking.

The sheer idiocy of smileys.

The future... you can't miss it!

The Time Is Now (Sing It Back).

Sharing motorcars is a necessity.

Creating cave-art on my iPad Pro.

Bison livers and personal computers.

Ben Carson: Straight Outta Compton.

American Woman (Stay Away From Me).

TV was going to change the world too, and it did.

Don 'Trump' MacCleans: American iSiS-Creampie.

The further destruction of the animal kingdom online.

Bernie Sanders: A Decent Future for A Decent America.

Saturday Night Live: Mick Huckabee & The Attractions: Pump It Up.

All we need to do is to go to the mountains, woods, and desert to pray.

The wise build bridges and the foolish build walls. ~ Nigerian proverb.

Illusion...

Connection.

Ending again.

Promised land.

Get the stretch!

Rock The Casbah.

Sleep on the floor.

Wait, there's more!

There is Radiation...

Windows and swans.

Designing mediocrity.

Countdown to ecstasy.

Space Invader Infinity.

Only nerds can be nerds.

Cyber attacking The Sun.

Life without the Internet.

Sleeping with the ancestors.

Who wants to be a millionaire?

Is the Internet the spread of evil?

Don't believe Jurassic World I Say.

Super sensing is a legitimate illness.

Johnny Depp est un gros dégueulasse.

Microsoft Office 3001: A Space Oddity.

Get the hell out of my life you moron robot!

Echo Beach and The Funnymen: Crocodiles.

Ask kindred spirits to bring you sweet dreams.

A library today is a collection of routines stored in a file.

Wisdom is like a baobab tree; no one individual can embrace it. ~ Akan proverb.

J'Accuzzi!

Inertia Creeps.

Visit your future.

Don't disk and drive!

Insane, insane again.

2 Minutes to Midnight.

Guitar Hero: Van Halen.

Man of Constant Sorrow.

Chatrooms are always dark.

Mixing Memory and Desire.

Veins of life, cables of death.

14 Hot Celebs who got really fat.

Monsters Ate My Birthday Cake!

Techno is the poetry of stupidity.

Where do you think you're going?

Je viendrai vomir sur vos tombes.

Everywhere it matters, we deliver.

Living the end of the world online.

Your phone is too smart for its own ass.

How wonderful it must be to be a seagull.

Morons and mormons stay at the Marriott Hotel.

Uncle Jeb's Extreme White Rice #(JamWithJeb).

And The Komodos Of Indonesia Love Donald Trump.

The Paste and Style Council: My every changing mood.

The Double Cheese Habsburger Royal Navy – Gay Night.

'I feel personally insulted, yes, I hate him, that German author.' Bill Gates III.

Introducing McAddy Trump, Ruler of the Quarter Pounder Habsburger Monarchy.

Uncle Ben's Carson White Rice Jazz Orchestra: Party on Plastic Neurosurgery Disasters.

Play Schubert to a muted pornflick and you're looking at Humanity Misunderstanding Itself.

Action.

Lady Writer.

PDF, RTF, LSD.

Hopi video games.

Hamburger Castle.

Keep us on the road.

Bush, botox, buttocks.

Curiosity killed the cat.

Read My Apple LipsInc.

I hammer you with silence.

United Colours of Skeletton.

Pop music is a 1000 Mozarts.

Love don't live here anymore.

You're currently off your rockets.

The Pueblo were there before you too.

We're Jebbin' right straight from yard...

Make America (The) Great (Dictator) Again.

Modern art has given us the appetite for trash.

You say goodbye, and I say Hello, is it me you looking for?

List, wrap, paste, save, attach and insert (#PainInTheAss).

Innocence, eXPERIENCE and darknet market file corruption.

In our face.

Silicon fools.

Fort minable!

Too hot to trot.

Obtain a refund (here).

God, World, Computer.

Like Me, Like Me, Like Me!

1 café, 21 clients, 19 laptops.

See, buy, fly, drink, eat, crash, die.

Can't judge Facebook by its cover...

The Internet is the viper of my eggs.

What happened to the human dream?

American by Birth. Asshole by Choice.

There's wifi in nature, but no nature in wifi.

One bus stand, 17 passengers, 16 smart phones.

The warlike, underground uprising of all bones.

You can skip this advertisement once in a lifetime.

The Super Size Me Bareback Gila Monster Club Texas.

Wrenched from the foul embrace from the rockstar who drools...

PopMart WeltDisneyland's Micky's Monkey Mousetraps all over.

The digital haves and the have-nots and the have-nothing-at-alls.

Tags, tools, toe-nails, Ice-Tea, Tinky Winkie, Tony Blair, teenagers.

Transmigration of digital souls into virtual turtles and online bears.

Bono Christ Bold Type Strip-On Hoodie € 499,99 (NEW TO STORE).

AXIOMERICA: Various | Ancient Heart and Fulani Music of the Gambia.

Get even.

Duplicate All.

Visions of China.

Software and saliva.

Life in the Mac Zone.

Giving birth in the ocean of e.

Hands across America online.

The Donald: Grab Them By The Riot!

Paleolithic, Byzantine, Cubist, Digital.

Now. Easy. Always. Forever. CREATE.

In Nature, butterflies are the real hackers.

The Kumbha Mela is a real collective experience.

Raptors, rockstars, Dino birds and ornithomimids.

Adam & Diana Ross: You Are Everything (Andy Aarhus Radio Edit).

The heart of the wise man lies quiet like limpid water. ~ Cameroon proverb.

Warkanoid IV, Looney Musk iTunes, Drill Sergeant Mindstrong, Crash Bash.

AC, BC, PC.

Watch video.

Combat Rock.

Consume to give.

Now you're gone.

Shareware is rare.

Malware from $299.

The new iPad Airbag.

Try gardening (I did).

Mania, tantra, Warhol.

Reinventing Humanity.

Money back guaranteed.

CYCLADES and cyclones.

Apple is not the only fruit.

Words apart, worlds apart.

Should I stay or should I go?

Mummies, yuppies, dummies.

The Experience of Connection.

Life is too short for computers.

The Boulevard of Broken Drums.

Nickels and dimes, tens and twenties.

Grandfather, help me to Walk the Talk.

Millionaires prefer to keep this video secret.

The Information Highway... how low does it get?

Notes, Stocks, Contacts, Settings, Reminders, Messages, Prophecies.

Apple Apple.

The Infernot.

Find (yourself).

Quit the Internet.

Buying in the blind.

I'm the Super Collider.

The World's local bank.

Dot communism is alive.

Protect Your Flies Today.

Jetzt Neues Handy Kaufen!

Steve Winwood: Higher Love.

We're all Mexicans these days.

Minnie Ripperton: Perfect Angel.

The Donald, King of the Bordermen.

Sinstagrammar for the multi-doomed.

Men have become the tools of their tools.

Rich, famous, paranoid, coked up and lonely.

The Bill and Calamity Jane Gates Foundation.

Sunglasses are Paris Hilton's favorite accessory.

Apple | Samsung: Small hands make big phones.

LSD-25, Windows OS-10, Shell Helix Ultra OW-30.

The Indians came way before the Dirt Brown Cowboys.

Running for president in pre-Colombus North America.

What Your Drinks Say About Your Personality Disorder.

There sure are some nasty chemists in our global village.

Those bisons once roamed where you now print burgers.

Selfie-sticks to beat the hell out of your personal provider.

Hunky Ian Dory & The Blogheads: Changes To Be Cheerful Part 3.

Ripping out my smoking kidneys, on top of the Internet Mountain.

Sunburnt, lonely, glazed, crunchy, sweet, crispy, bitter, angry, sour.

Buffalo Bill killed 4.282 bison in 18 months, and 68 bison in 8 hours.

The real problem is not whether machines think but whether men do.

A Massive Attack of Unfinished Sympathy for the real world we live in.

Brillo soap pads afloat on The Great Pre-Columbus North American River.

William Henry Gates III was an American scout, bison hunter and showman...

I.M. Long Wolf, Paul Eagle Star, White Star Ghost Dog, Surrounded-by-the-Enemy.

Everybody gets so much information all the time that they loose their common sense.

The new electronic independence re-creates the world in the image of the global village.

Call me.

I Me Mine.

Leave no reply.

Mr. Wonderful.

Hans ARPANet.

See, view, watch.

Praise and blame.

Remove all screws.

Lots of free storage.

More party, less fun.

The Great Unknown.

Spamsung and deleted.

NeoGeo Battle Coliseum.

Prince: The Love We Make.

www... where eagles can't fly.

Stiff Necked Fools (take it all).

A PC from the land of the wolf.

Local talk leads to global gossip.

A net-community has no shaman.

Change your orientation (Drag II).

Yes Sir, I can google, google woogle...

Uncle Samsung Wants YOU for OS Army!

Super size me, myselfies & Donkey Tramp.

Fuck Google, Ask me | Fuck me, ask Google.

Digital wallpaper... one of us will have to go.

Web hosting, weight watching, Cosmic Slop.

Child-labor uncovered in Apple's supply chain.

Unwatched TV Shows and prehistoric funeral rites.

Damned souls love travelling fiberglass without moving.

It's annoying enough when it works, but boy if it doesn't...

Will our children's children's children still need each other?

A man who uses force is afraid of reasoning. ~ Kenyan proverb.

Imagine... a Dino Woodstock Festival in Mezozoic North America.

Running out of battery, running out of battery, running out of battery.

The Great Mammarian Macintosh Milkshake Microsoft Mystery Tour.

Ignorance is the curse of God, knowledge is the wing wherewith we fly to Heaven.

Big Fleetwood MacDonald Trump's Presidential Campaign Anthem: Go your own way.

Add credit.

Being There.

The Byte Poets.

Design yourself.

Silicon Follywood.

Doc, I'm Bipolaroid.

I believe in a better way.

When the wild wind blows.

We're up all night to get lucky.

The Net: sExclusion from Bliss.

Looking at cave art restores the brain.

America's top communists of all time.

Child-labor isn't working (it's slavery).

The musical laziness of internet playlists.

An Oscar is the final insult to any artist's career.

Afro-American Bushmen vs. Wall Street brokers.

When the eagles scream at the foot of the Internet Mountain.

Wherever the machine is, there is always the abyss and the void.

Nature, Todd Rundgren's Utopia and the Garden of Earthly Delights.

USAXIOMERICA: Gnawa Music of Marrakesh | Night Spirit Masters.

For The Love of The Savage God, folk-music, spatial poetry and Choco Pops.

Infiltrated, colonialised, drugged, penetrated, kidnapped, sunburnt, paranoid and alone.

Shame.

Jungle Speed.

USALLSDeceit.

The Fear Factory.

Get wasted online.

Gamers Anonymous.

The Age of the Selfie.

Hallucination Engine.

See it all like never before.

The World and Ourselfies.

iMac + iDraw + iFeel nothing.

Another 90 bucks for a f* cable.

OneDrive is enough for all of us.

Think different: DISCONNECT.

Life is precious, virtuality is not.

Wreck on the Information Highway.

Redneck Bull. Save up to 0% Energy.

System Preferences: Language & Religion.

And now they do what they told you they would.

Where revolutionary spirit is bought for very little.

I tried to drown my iPhone 6, but it is still working.

A girl knows about his disk-drive from the way he eats.

Einstein Coffee, Bollinger Ice Tea Brut, Red Bull Grand Cru.

Connecting with schizoid, murderous bankemployees online.

Accommodation of the personal computer in the American family.

Brilliant remixes, exuberant production, big hooks and suicide rates worldwide.

Hoop Dreams.

This is not a Mac.

Unplug your soul.

Around the world.

Selected writings...

Will my iLife degrade?

Pornstars have no bones.

Take a walk on the timeline.

Zombie Drive, Voodoo Dice.

Add up to something smaller.

The internet is psychic terror.

Subscribe without commenting.

Here are stories we think you'll love.

Nasty nerds, gumbo geeks, fuzzy freaks.

Trump is a psychotic pop-phenomenon.

36 ridiculous selfies seriously gone wrong.

...or do you want to come with me and change the world...?

Home Sweet Home Obamalabama (Chicago Library Edit).

Driven to discs.

Globally trusted.

Nachos and laptops.

Connective depression.

Bursting the banks of e.

Fame – Who's to Blame?

Young capital, old game.

iDrinks and PC-dinners.

Coffins and blockbusters.

Water versus electronics.

We won't see the end of it.

Turning my digital stomach.

I'm pushing my wheel of love.

Your partner in climax solutions.

The Stone Age did not know Hell.

The rich eradicating poverty, great.

Single shot, double pounder, triple X.

Chi-mails, con-shells and burrito wraps.

Cage Against The Machine: eVil eMpire.

The Internet does not make a good story.

I'm just giving ya all a popdate here, folks.

The revolt in the Kellogg's Skull Cathedral.

Visit the future, live your dreams, play to sin.

Brown sugar bears no catch no salmon online.

Redbone regalia for Tribal Spirit Fashionistas.

LSDisney Worldwars in post Stone Age America.

We're always in front of it, they're always behind it.

My mind is on fire, halfway on the Internet Mountain.

The Animal Bone Graveyard in the post Burger Society.

Motherboarding terrorists (Welcome to the Drone Zone).

Artsy Apps for phoney iPads and NRApple Mac Airstrikes Pro.

Digital rock art, electro choco pops and post-coital Bluetooth-aches.

Buffalo Bootsy & Bison Wild West Unity Funk Band: Chocolate City.

Megyn Kellogg's & CNNRAmerican All Stars: Jumpin' Apple Jackflash.

Humanity Astray: We can't even slaughter our own pineapples anymore.

Coca Cola Live, Coca Cola Light Verse and The Coca Cola Zero Point of No Return.

The Righteous Brothers: Jebb Tide (So I Rush To Your Side, Like The Oncoming Tide).

Shop – Act – Learn.

Where's my water?

Get into the action!

Phishing to be clever.

We need a resolution.

DOS is the root of all evil.

Hi, Hilarius, and goodbye.

That guy is so full of spam.

Take me to the wild places.

Tell me that I'm streaming...

Everybody got their something.

Surfing is Our Heavenly Dwelling.

African phones are thousands of years old.

A homepage is where there is one to love us.

View extended Nigeria weather forecast on Yahoo Weather.

Get the latest Bangladesh news headlines from Yahoo News.

e Suicide.

Massage Me.

Wait a minute!

Doors Of The Mind.

Cellphones can wait.

Living inside a drum.

me@sacred-texts.com.

Are you Hilarius Hofstede?

There's a time for every star.

Microsoft Clearwater Revival.

Videogames are hardly playful.

Spidersleep, cyberspace, psychopomp.

e-Hope prolongs the torments of Man.

Know your computer before it knows you.

Howlin' in the wind, howlin' in the dust of e.

Talented Apple users from around the world.

Forgot to check out again and again and again.

Bangladesh news headlines from Yahoo News.

Ronald MacDonald Trumpadelic P-Fucked we are.

iPad mini 3 Disney princesses dressed to kill Bill G.

Mac Power Soul, Microsoft people and Funkhansa Flight Instructions.

Electroplankton, protected passwords and cataleptic trans states of tv-evangelists.

My TV Shows, All My Flies, Zen Pinball, e-tropolis, War of the Worlds, Killer Instinct Gold.

Scare Me.

Another life.

Bits in space.

Lost To Tech.

Lick and share.

In full remission.

All is (not) dream.

Freedom to create.

Conservative, moi?

(WHAT) About Us.

The Abyss Odyssey.

Simple, safe, secure.

Hope of Deliverance.

Déja Vu (a 1000 times).

Joining the cosmic fire.

Eternal fame, everyday.

Elsewhere is otherwise.

Children of the Damned.

Twisted, tweeted, twittered.

The War Against Anti-Funk!

Evil Quarter Pounder with Choice.

A digital boomerang never returns.

The sun sets but doesn't rise online.

Uncle Jeb's Rice-Pops is killer food!

We may got our wires crossed again.

What the hell is wrong with a stamp?

Arabic Speaking Internet Infiltration...

Welcome to My World (John Travolta).

Charlie & The Foxconn Suicide Factory.

The Karaoke Revolution Party Program.

On the Net you never feel really welcome.

AWB: I got work to do! (We got work to do!).

There ain't no smallest part of what is small.

The feeling you're being sold something, all the time.

Uncle Ben Johnson & Johnson's e-Soap Circus Part 333.

The Western BBQ Habswhopper Monarchy Mausoleum.

Gimmee gimmee gimme gimmee gimmee gimmee that cake!

Cyber-security small satellite dish systems called ripe for hacking?

Paul 'Pot' McCarthy: Choice is a McChicken with Wings in America...

Get the latest news on health, Harper's Bazar, nutrition, shitcans and fitness.

Zwei Habsburger King Red Hot Chili Onion Pepper Twister Fries Bitte Schön!

Compton's Tomato Soup and optical head-mounted display of genitals of goats.

Donald Trump & The Lynrd Skynrd GOP Brides of Frankenstein: Sweet Home Alabama.

The Curse.

iSOLATION.

The Detector.

Quality Quick.

System Shock 2.

The eTon Rifles.

Exit planet DOS.

Totem and Yahoo.

Right off the hook.

High Art, low taxes.

Vinyl sounds better.

Simplify your journey.

Logos, insults, slogans.

Tim Coo Coo Cachook!

The White House Album.

Back to the past, what else?

Monitoring goes both ways.

Nothing to text home about.

The IMG-Spot Photo Tornado.

Ich will ein Fisch im Wasser sein.

Making Plans For Nigela Lawson.

With or without youtube, but without.

Steve & Hugo Ballmer: California Dada.

On Ego Beach where I sat down and whopped.

Purple haze, pink hysteria and orange hurricanes.

Plus more deals down the long and dwindling road.

Deers eating from decision trees can become suicidal.

Introducing the Paranoid Android Planet PC Tablet Hell!

Ensuring freedom, security and grow in our digital world.

McSpielburgers, Kinosaur leg-bones and Internet Live States.

We're Jebbin', Jebbin', Jebbin' (Bob Marley Ambient Dub Mix).

Los Beatles, Yellow Mellow Submarine, Komm Gib Mir Deine Hand.

Dionysos, not Jobs, Bono, Musk, Cook, Gates, Schmidt, Clooney, Zuckerberg.

Black Sea Medusa.

Select, sling and shoot.

Prelude to the end of the game.

Peak performances all day long.

Purple Hayes: Hot Buttered Soul.

James Brown: Deus Sex Machina.

You do have a common Client Interface.

Paroles complètes sur Google Play Music.

I'm The Great Microsoft Mystery Shopper.

Dr. Trump-N-Furter meets Dr. Caligari in America!

Fifty shades of filth (Lars Von Trier Final Cut-Up Method).

We're Jebbin'… to think that Jebbin' was a thing of the past…

Fling all these things away; live as your forefathers did before you.

Jay Zizi, Mulholland Google Drive, PowerPuff Girls – Bad Mojo Mojo.

Amazing pompadours, quiffs and other underground hairstyle inspirations.

We all live in a yellow soup terrine, yellow soup terrine, yellow soup terrine…

Yahoo Parenting, Fantasy The Nice Remix Perfume and Rubber Soul Recovery.

Frank Sinatra: Jebb Tide (I Can Feel, You Are Love, You Are Real, Really Mine).

Go Nutz!

Cry baby cry.

Bugs 'n Balls.

Jurassic Arse.

We want more.

Dress Code Red.

In the real world.

In the loop of Fame.

You got what it takes.

Achtung Baby Bubba!

Message from a drum.

The McCarthy Burger.

Does your mother know?

Jihadi Jennifer Likes This!

Psychiatres Sans Frontières.

In Yahoo Beliefs and Rituals.

Stay Strong Water Protectors!

One Flew Over The Google Clan.

Giant Elk skeletons and storage options.

Americans are dinosaurs in a WASP body.

Campbell's Critique of Pure Reason Tomato Soup.

By the bush of Buffalo she said she was a magic mama.

Launching the iPhone McDSM-5 in the nude, boys & girgoyles.

Wisdom is not like money to be tied up and hidden. ~ Akan proverb.

George Clinton's Mothership is in the Smithsonian, thinking it's an igloo.

The New President of the United States of America: Reverend John Holmes.

Rip out my monkey intestines you bunch of fat, famous, fabulous pop-raptors!

William 'Bootsy' Burroughs: The Naked Lunchadelic Zillatronic Age has come.

Rewriting Warhol: Campbell's Space Shooter Blitzouppatronic Bass Blobaganza.

'Microsoft Mon Amour is a disturbing effort to unmask our great Valley.' Bill Gates.

Gran-Turismo 3 A-Spec, 20th-century electro-Shockly and cosmic noise funk waves.

Coca-Cola Pro-Life and Redbull Pro-Death (Particularly children under the age of 5).

Bactrosaurus – the duck-billed dinosaur, family management and Internet side effects.

Buffalo Bill Gates & The Crazy Cajun Cakewalk Band: Be What's Next (Bison Club Mix).

Roger Robot.

Empty Trash.

Ronald Tramp.

Genes and chips.

La Grande Illusion.

The Petroleum Son.

Genius starts at $99.

We are the solutions.

Hippies with a business plan.

Dream if you wanna go faster.

Life already is a disaster dump.

The virtual Path is not the highest.

Sticks in a bundle are unbreakable.

Come and sit on my laptop my love.

Banksy-Moon is an excellent con-artist.

Many call themselves StyleWriters today.

The Internet... a fresh start for Humanity.

Space was born from the hip-bone of Time.

Plastic surgery, web hosting, weight watching.

Population, World Population, Real World Population.

The collapse of the prefrontal cortex due to 24/7 onlineness.

You do not teach the paths of the forest to an old gorilla. ~ Congolese proverb.

Go to settings.

Flip, flop and fly.

Bite of Las Vegas.

How To Be A Genius.

The Devil's been busy.

I'll have what she's having.

The 10 unknown Google tricks.

Don't Stop Till You Get Enough!

The Facebook logo is my new home.

Oh God, I Am The American Dream!

I go to the balls and then ring the bell.

The B-Movie: Bush, Blair, Berlusconi.

Sometimes you dot – sometimes you com.

Force feeding monks, force quitting clerics.

Bobbi Kristina Houston, we have a problem.

Microsoft or the Anatomy of Industrial Order.

Calvin Klein ONE (RED) Edition Eau de Toilet.

Tutu, I have a feeling were not in Kansas anymore.

Major Tim Cookle, narcissistic personality and the Rainbow.

With sensory loss.

Half man – half disc.

Highway 51 Revisited.

Finding Flint Eastwood.

Factual accuracy disputed.

With Use Disorder, severe.

A Zombie Stole My Toaster.

Our exploding hearts online.

Hades is the Disco of Exploitation.

Buying an iPhone: A season in hell.

Eisbein, Sauerkraut, Bulimia, Obezos.

The Internet will create a new psychiatry.

Uncle Jeb Wants You: GOPPLE DA GEEK.

You get rid of the bad guys by using our guns.

Depression, poverty and hassle-free bill payment.

Punk, voodoo, Internet, theosophy, José Mourinho.

The Online Museum of Modern Miserable Mediocrity.

The Vodafone 3G-Spot Longle Dongle Carcrash Affair.

US porn on a smartphone in a cornfield in Afghanistan.

The Uncle Jamazon.Cumba Zumba Bossa-Nova-Zemblast!

Apple Lips Inc. Suckerburger with (do) fries (pull that shake?)

Diagnostic and Statistical McManual of McMental McDisorders.

All we have to do now, is take these lies and make them true somehow.

Dart points, knife blades, tomahawks and free antivirus scan in progress.

Arthur Rimbaud & Le Pays Où Revent Les Fourmis Vertes All-Stars: Absinth.

Redbone, Prehistoric Rhythm, Jimi Hendrix, Monica Lewinsky, George Clinton.

Space Safari, Cruise Ship Vacation games and giant South-American river turtles.

Rewriting Warhol: Joseph Campbell's Condensed McChicken 'n McDumplings Soup.

I did it myWay.

Money matters.

Concrete jungle.

Come In Handy!

Byte up your life.

Intimacy has died.

A PC knows no God.

Amazon is a river wild.

Jesus Christ Megabyte.

Smashing my computer.

Frank Zappa: Them or us.

Hitachi Cheese and Onion.

Born from a mortal mother.

Gates, Windows, peepholes.

Virtuality has no framework.

Lord of the Heavenly Web Hosts.

Neanderthal Man was connected.

Explore the World not the Internet.

A salty rebirth from the salty bones.

You have no credit to make this call.

Microsoft Mon Amour: Unfriendly Fire.

The driving force behind hybrid warfare.

There's neither Space or Time in virtuality.

Video games are the toys of mass destruction.

I did not use to check my mailbox 15 times a day.

Bill Gates: L'Homme à Deux Visages: Day & Night.

By the time the fool has learned the game, the players have dispersed.

Apache.

Close X.

iGenesis.

Get A Grip.

No way out.

Save a virgin.

Life in the now.

The USA-Bomb.

Spice up your life.

Really Amezosoic!

Reachability is now.

Planet Google Earth.

Machine of the Year.

Shop Now, Think Later.

Protection We All Need.

Like, Follow, Disappear.

Presidents and dinosaurs.

Running out of FaceTime.

Limitation is a good thing.

Vous n'avez encore rien vu.

We want more, always more.

The song is still the samsung.

Carry me home to see my kin.

The world ends with dot com.

Wind, Water, Weather Report.

Passion for pioneering the End.

Somebody took the words away.

Cardinals do not enjoy cybersex.

Money is too tight to mention too.

You ain't nothing but a hound dog.

Everybody wants to rule the world.

No boundaries to the madness of e.

Tony Blair Witch Vol. 2: Coffin Rock.

Onlineness, insomnia and soultravel.

Shipping, safety, security and online slander.

The Flintstones, The Simpsons, The Clintons.

John Clavin Klein's Naked Touch ft. Joan Smalls.

The Bytes of Reason versus the Bones of Madness.

U2 Tour Unisex Full Zip Hooded Sweatshirt $749.00.

Utopian orderings at the psychiatric facility nearest to you.

On Creativity and the Unconsciousness: Twerk it like Miley!

USA: The Will To Powder (White Powder Dillinger Club Mix).

Starbucks, starfish, coffee and revised criteria for eating disorders.

Rebel Heart, Bieber's Purpose and additional changes to Paraphiliac Disorders.

Size?

Krashzachstan.

London Calling.

Popes don't cry.

Watch yer sign?

The Digital Abyss.

The Big Mac Menu.

Steering the World.

The Wizard of OS10.

Get it now on iDrones!

Falling through the Net.

WiMaximise your mysteries.

The Big Silver Money Machine.

As Internet penetration increases...

Wake up and connect before coffee.

The privileged always make it home.

From digital divide to digital inequality.

Access for non-Hispanic, white collar hyenas.

Expanding education, good jobs and better health?

Devil devil whatcha know? Devil devil you're gonna go!

Karl Schlagerfeld ft. Heino & Bono Christ: Germanic Reggae.

Between the online and the offline, the digital haves and have-nots.

The Ronald McLaing Anti-Psychiatric Double Pounder HabsBurger works wonders!

The Wire.

Talk To Me.

Smiley Zyprexa.

Try it FREE for 5 days!

Coffee, starfish and wifi.

Something's Gotta Give.

Who is John Calvin Klein?

How fast does a bison run?

Send Pere Ubu songs to your cell.

You are about to be redirected to: America.

Lowlands Gorilla Paw and Updated Disorders.

Gaming compulsively for the need of a new Utopia.

Research, treatment, diagnoses and capital punishment.

Navy Seals, DSM-5 Task Force and the invasion of Baghdad.

Sly & The Family Stone-Age Europeans were the first to set foot in Stone Age America.

Who's Horus?

All goes down.

The Silicon Valley: MACCA.

Shopping is the new church.

May the world be rid of stars.

When the demon is at your door.

Time is not money, time is Time.

Fred Wesley: Funk For Your Ass.

Last Night The DJ Saved My Life.

Zoophiliacs can go and f* themselves.

Adding a phone number to my account.

Still having the dignity of having no money.

Normal people going about their daily lives.

Your teenage daughter naked online, forever.

Taking the cat for a walk (The Fashion Years).

Access for those who are already ahead in life.

A French kiss is an eternal variation on a theme.

Great Spirit, let me live my life in a spiritual way.

Si vous voulez une saucisse, c'est en libre service!

The History of Inequity (Lauren Hillary Clinton...?)

One is only beautiful through suffering or innocence.

Yves Saint Laurent and Jimi Hendrix shared bipolarity.

The Owl of Minerva only flies at Saturday Night Live-time.

WorldOnDope.

Broken English.

Gone with the wind.

Remember the beach?

Technology comes shiny.

Web, sites and brick gods.

The Great Gateway Keeper.

Naked in front of the computer.

The sun is only a hard-disc wide.

Good fish you find in the harbour.

If I see the word 'free' once more...

Desktops, notebooks and elephant birds.

And where does the game controller live?

The harder they come, the harder they fall.

A long expected love-letter on the doormat...

Drawing on iPads: The Wet Hockney Dream.

Windows everywhere, but not a house for rent.

Creation was like Program Creation, they think.

Sirens, cheerleaders, prophets, chief executives.

'Hofstede is a wonderful historian.' Terry Jones.

On Skype, everybody looks like Cross-Eyed Mary.

Reindeers waiting in line for the rebirth of the world.

The Information Highway never hits a beautiful coastline.

Virtual Reichs for faceless creeps, faceless Reichs for virtual creeps.

Shop now.

Shiva Vibe.

We'll be gone.

Don't be cruel.

Peerless in Gaza.

Addiction to bite.

One Phone Nation.

Right on the money.

Maggot World Brain.

Maggot Brain World.

LifeStyle and iNfinity.

Avatar: Into The Inferno.

Let Nature do the talking.

We are not one, thank God.

A Quickfix (is what is needed).

The Internet is Otherworld Illusion.

You don't need charisma to start a digital sect.

The Jackson 5 ft. Elvis Presley: Heartbreak Hotel.

Everybody has something to share except me and my monkey.

eBaywatch presents: Silicon Paradise feat. Spamela Anderson.

U2, Patti Smith & Egos of Deaf Cattle: People Have The Powder.

3rd World-Warkanoid Android Apps for printing patient-groups.

TV-evangelism, naming of the bones and formal thought disorder.

Alaskaos.

Gros Ventres.

Bipolar regions.

I got buffalosized.

Behind a snow-drift.

Sweet: Off The Record.

Robots and hamburgers.

In the shadow of the rockies.

With horns of six-foot spread...

The Teardrop Explodes: Wilder.

Killing the game of e from the saddle.

Keith Moon: Two Sides Of The Phone.

You come with a cat and you call it a robot.

Sarah Palin riding (a) fossil bison of Alaska.

Donald Trump, Germanic reggae and buffalo slaughter.

Who goes out hunting with no dogs, comes home with no robots.

The further we travelled west, the more plentiful became the buffalo.

Uncle SIMM.

All You Creeps.

Good day in hell.

Apples and apes.

Biting the bitcoin.

You're under arrest.

Margot's Word Brain.

Hard To Concentrate.

Hearts + Minds + Dollars.

My Cart (0) CHECKOUT.

Downtown money waster.

Adam's first bank-account.

The bulimia of being online.

The bin's too big without you.

Online nobody takes a shower.

The rocky rape of William Blake.

The Apple Human Rights Watch?

I'll be glad to see the back of it all!

Arizona Wind Spirit Rage Outburst.

Get the latest Afghanistan news on Yahoo!

App, Life, dream, choice, download, suicide.

50 Things You Didn't Know About Your Hair.

Every generation is known for something indeed.

Dissociative Amnesia, flat screens, nature scenes.

MacAir, Divine Being, Google Glass, Cosmic Mountain.

Porn statistics (Alaska) and some buffalo characteristics.

3-Disney-World Perfect and Deluxe CD-set & T-Shirt (Bundle 1) €331,00.

Miserably poor in Manchester but hoping to be a rockstar one day soon after I turn 14.

Donate.

Off limits.

Sir Snowden.

Notify me not.

Living in a box.

We heart it not.

Electronic Nuba.

Away away away.

All together now!

A PC has no antlers.

This Doodle's Reach.

She's so dot common!

I feel so low, I feel low.

Damn and be damned.

Some kind of madness.

TC Matic Droidcast 43.

Stones, stingers, services.

Dying a mainstream death.

The Holy AppleScriptures.

Optimising my mediocrity.

A never-ending nightmare.

Creating problems together.

Even in the quietest moments.

Your light in a world of change.

Remember Erich PHonHäcker?

Virtuality leads to phantom pain.

Hairdressers of the World Unite!

Offline, where you can feel so free.

You always have the sample option.

A virtual vampire tends to like milk.

Online unconsciousness as symbolic death.

Prince & 3rdEyeGirl: Something in the water.

Crosstown Traffic: Jimi Hendrix & Post-War Pop.

The Silicon Chip Circus of Totalitarian Take-Over.

Not to know which day, month or year you are born.

The split second your life stayed the same as it ever was.

When you're ready for your booty to do its duty on the dance floor.

Paris Hilton's shoe collection, sacrifice of goats and other social phobias.

Earth, fire, 7UP, giga-bite, Pepsi Light and pathological meditation on bones.

She's a fan.

Tolstoi in Texas.

Ape Escape Academy.

Hardware Pour Hommes.

Preferring Gogol to Google.

Let's... get the f* out of here!

Virtual livers, digital kidneys.

Lenny Kravitz: Living in fear.

Licking stamps... I remember!

Paul Weller: I wish upon a star.

The trivial pursuit of happiness.

Randy Newman: Little Criminals.

And a digital Third World as well!

This computer is a dead computer.

Why the hell is it not working now?

Easyjet, Virgin Air, Air Cunnilingus.

Prozac, e-masonry and night terrors.

Lenny Kravitz: Black & Red America.

Paedophiles can go and kill themselves.

To facilitate e-banking, tell us your life story.

Liquid Jesus... wash me over... wash me clean...

We don't have anything you need in stock right now!

Somewhere between psychedelics and an astute business instinct.

Open Source wellness, celebrity perfumes and spirit language disorder.

Yahoo Style, Viagrasoft Windows, psychoactive eagle and origins of shamans.

Britney Spears Fantasy Eau de Toilet, bone sacrifice and ecstatic initiation rites.

NO MORE!

Let's enlarge.

Sign In Stranger.

Balzac in Baltimore.

A long and happy life.

Of iBooks and impalas.

Dead souls all the same.

Underclocking wintertime.

Banging the bricks of Reason.

Laptops, lungfish and lemurs.

Tagged, lost and downgraded.

That lady is so bitmapped, man!

Hell... just switch on your computer.

Hide, turn off and don't kill yourself.

Virtuality, psychosis and human nature.

'Bono owes all of us a fiver.' Johnny Rotten.

Apple's G-Spotlight Search (Set sounds and vibrations).

The Rise and Fall of the Modern Machine in our lives, yesterday today and tomorrow.

What now?!

Carrot Crazy.

No sympathy.

So much trouble.

The Discourse of i.

New ways to connect.

The Nature of Money.

Scuba-diving into byte.

Halliburton Dreaming...

I'm busy notworking mama.

White powder, black market.

What it is to be human, online.

The outline of one's inner life-story.

Demons, techno music and video games.

System Preferences: Spotlight on Otis Redding.

Living a life of constant change and make-overs.

The Apple Genius Bar... where are the bloody drinks?

You can not get to the library of Ashurbanipal by mouse.

Goodnight Bill. Goodnight Steve. Goonight Tim. Goonight. Ta ta.

Paranoia, surveillance, Starbucks Coffee, and Bison Caravan habitat resurrection.

LSD, loving-kindness, Monica Lewinsky and Uncle Jeb's White Rice House aspirations.

Go for a walk.

Know the lingo.

Trending Tropics.

The Enslaved Mind.

Modify your account.

In Twitter BIO space.

Do you wanna dance?

Noah was a surfer too.

WeFollow The Master.

Water of Life (forget about e).

Are you up for the down stroke?

Living inside your online bank account.

Viral bonuses for binge-drinking bankers.

Womb goddesses and digital pregnancies.

Coming in handy for finding my lost phone.

Tag your FB friends in your worst nightmares.

Take me to the place I love take me all the way.

Use cookies, share information, ruin your reputation.

Give it away give it away give it away give it away now.

Social Oompha's Loompha's and random friends invites.

Experiencing a UFO visit while driving from Detroit to Toronto.

400 million people watching Ronaldo MacDonaldo Trampère Ubus.

TwitPic, Thyrax, Qwitter, Twitterific, Pinterest, terrified out of my wits.

Marketing anti-depressants, Facebook purity add-ons and fake celebrity death reports.

Dial PPP.

Here To Stay.

In a word, no.

Bowling alone.

Speed is a drug.

Primal Carnage.

Praise and blame.

The Book of Jobs.

Shareware is rare.

Remove all screws.

Money money money.

Blood, SWAT & Chips.

We want Armani back!

Mein Feuer, I can swim!

Money back guaranteed.

Most things don't happen.

Dark side of the bright life.

Words apart, worlds apart.

Computing leads to obesitas.

Don't touch what you can't afford.

Not all is fish that comes to the net.

Let's go deeper (One crime at the time).

Computer anxiety seeps into everyday lives.

Treeview Components for birds of paradise.

Space Did Not Exist Before Gagarin Entered It.

Jeb!, Bushvipers, Instant Jell-O, Latoya Jackson.

Thin Lizzy Taylor, Fatboy Carlos Slim, Duck-Billed Gates.

Notes, Stocks, Contacts, Settings, Reminders, Messages, Prophecies.

Joseph Bowie & The Defunkt Anti-Funk Funk Division: Knuckle Sandwich.

Ignorance is the curse of God, experience is the wing wherewith we fly to Heaven.

Heal The World.

The Wrath of God.

Free computer help?

Why You Wanna Trip On Me?

Watch me watch me watch me!

Who was born on my birthday?

A monkey wrench in the works.

The story seems to be false, really.

Peter Greenaway: Drowning By Pixels.

Changing the world, sharing the earth.

Rock and Roll Hell of Fame: Inductees.

You're wrecking your brains boys 'n girls.

Chasing sheep is best left to the shepherds.

Brazil gun violence and Dino Birdman statistics.

Mud turtles with tiger feet shouldn't throw cakes.

Just stop pressuring me (makes me wanna scream).

A journey of a thousand sites begins with a single click.

The Boss, Top Dog, Hugo Boss, She's The Boss, iBomber3.

Getting information off the Internet is like taking a drink from a fire hydrant.

The World's a woman in her prime, and the Web an old man dying from his sex-addiction.

On Twitter we get excited when someone follows us, in real life we get scared and run away.

'Microsoft Mon Amour is a lovely mix of English sensibility and Danish pragmatism.' Time Out.

Everywhere.

Adopt a bison.

Game of Dhrones.

Time is the real killer.

Making a case for new disorders.

Read more about our underwear.

Frequently Asked Questions: Bison.

U2: ONE Pour Hommes, Eau de Toilet.

Luxury gadgets for folks in need of the opposite.

Socks, software, swimwear, loungewear, Lounge Lizards.

Britney Spears, Simon Cowell, Adam Clayton, Che Guevara.

Millions of bison thundering through The Beverly Hills Hotel.

Hi there!... I'm Nikita Lauda on the Information Highway to Hell!

Refugees please note, changing country will empty out your basket.

Rewriting Warhol: Compton's Tomato Soup Cans 11 times in black & white.

No restraints should limit the degree of change between DSM-5 and past editions...

Boyzone, Stranglers, Take That, Sex Pistols, OneDirection, Joy Division, Backstreet Boys.

Muck & Co.

Fade to grey.

Into the trees.

No surrender.

Copy the world.

Get it here and now!

Someday it will come down.

With one bullet – two robots!

New World Order: Blue Monday.

Fast delivery, free returns, money back.

When is the digital rut you beautiful people?

André Agassi, Johnny Lydon, Roger Federer.

Britain Got Talent: Simon Cowell & Art Garfunkel.

NEWS: David Beckham takes his kids to Legoland!

Gold digging inside Joseph Campbell's Soup Bubbles.

New Edition, Zawinul's Weather Report, New Kids On The Block.

The Nordic Stone Age and Björn Borg's Iconic Underwear Collection.

Microsoft Mon Amour: Transcending the ceremony and ritual of religion.

Information, human knowledge and Divine knowledge among the Greeks.

Bison funk blizzards across the Presidential Election Campaign Trail 2016.

Westlife, Fischer Z, Boyz II Men, Mötorhead, Jonas Brothers, The Mothers of Invention.

Really?

All by my side.

Lovely juju juju.

Soft morning city.

Slow Food Coming.

Fender is the night.

Special characters...

The Best, or nothing.

Hold The Line Part 3.

An online Aristocracy?

Dancin' in the moonlight.

The Information Railway.

Nervous, nervous, nervous.

Offline, just for the sake of it.

The Internet starts with YOU!

Walking barefoot into Oblivion.

George and Sly on the hog 2012.

We own the reading of this world.

Where there's smoke, there is water.

The Great Taming of the Inner Wild.

Mutiny on the Microsoft Mothership.

P-Funk: The Drones of Dr. Funkenstein.

Looking like Moonie and George Clooney.

A kitchen-dog is never a good robot-hunter.

Sun Ra, Moondog, George Clinton, Donald J. Trump.

The Internet is the perfect mask for anyone malignant.

Virtual reconstructions: Lascaux, Stonehenge, Acropolis.

D'Angelo: The Black Tornado of RnF (Rhythm and Funk)

'Microsoft Mon Amour: Its truths are open to all.' Guardian.

Rhythm killers, Army Arrangement, Anti-Funk Funk Division.

Happy Hour: Gordon's Gin, Chanel No. 5, Esso Diesel, Mojito Syrup, lemon zest.

Lots of free storage.

More party, less fun.

Whaling For Words.

Get yer ya's ya's out!

I Played My Red Guitar.

Bend over like Beckham.

Konrad Zuse's Z1, on the ONE!

OneDrive is enough for all of us.

Think different: DISCONNECT.

A net-community has no shaman.

Looking at the world, and ourselfies.

BloodSugarStaxMagic: Purple Hayes.

System Preferences: Language & Religion.

Uncle Samsung Wants YOU for O.S. Army!

Where revolutionary spirit is bought for very little.

Microsoft Mon Amour and the Road to Rock'n Roll Part 3.

View extended Nigeria weather forecast on Yahoo Weather.

Get the latest Bangladesh news headlines from Yahoo News.

Imagine... a Dino Woodstock Festival in Mezozoic North America.

Accommodation of the personal computer in the American family.

The Great Mammarian Macintosh Milkshake Microsoft Mystery Tour.

Sony Xperia z3 compact, Alligator Death Comet Tiki and The Heinz Kaleidoscope.

We'll be known as those crazy generations flushing their faeces with drinking water.

Eradicating e.

The American.

Wuda Cuda Shuda.

Appriver, downhill.

Bizziniss to dizziness.

The Heavy Water War.

Face your art, America!

Secrecy, secrecy, secrecy.

Force-feeding bad music.

There's money in it, it seems

Microsoft Unification Church.

Humanity has become clientèle.

Where have all the flowers gone?

All is well that ends the Internet.

These Roots Are Made For Fonkin'.

Standing on the verge of getting it on.

Coca Cola Zero Appellation Controlée.

I was born into an extraordinary world.

Can't read my own handwriting anymore.

Online advertisement for muted Youtubers.

We do NOT face the same questions everyday.

'Microsoft Mon Amour is an essential read.' Christine Lagarde.

Yasmine Hamdan – Hal (official music video) #JimJarmusch Edit.

Hell in One.

Circus Chaos.

Talk about us.

The Last Story.

This War Of Mine.

Let them have byte!

The Occultinationals.

It's Nature you stupid.

This is your last chance.

It ends where you leave it.

Mental oceans do rise online.

Get those smileys outta ma face!

Post-Pop War I, Post-Pop War II.

That Nature is our virtual reality.

Polio eradication is the amazing effort.

3.5000.000.000 skeletons in the closet of e.

Reduction of sexuality, destruction of sensuality.

Ahmed Fakroun – Yo Son/Sahranin (Edit De Prince Language).

Let's Spittify!

Botox your brain.

Man and his God: e.

Hades comes home.

There's a riot goin' on.

Vibes from the Scribes.

Take me to the wild places Part 51.

Ronald Reagan, Nancy Spungen and I.

The Meanderthals knew about fluctuation.

Il y a plein de moutons dans le ciel, regarde.

Body surfing salty waves, there's nothing like it.

Miley Zyprexa & Red Wrecking Bull All-Stars: Let It Bleed.

My Creator, let me love. Let me put into action the love dominos.

Mac Power Soul, Microsoft people and Funkhansa Flight Instructions.

The answer my friend, is flowing in the mind, the answer is flowing in the mind.

Electroplankton, protected passwords and cataleptic trans states of tv-evangelists.

My TV Shows, All My Flies, Zen Pinball, e-tropolis, War of the Worlds, Killer Instinct Gold.

Prime Music.

Stuff like that.

Wait a minute!

More categories.

You might also like...

Beehives go bankrupt too.

Scarcity in a scarred world.

Fossils, origins and innovations.

A city is an archipel gone wrong.

Bushmen, serpents, bird, tree, PC.

Time is like a river, the Internet is not.

Meret Oppenheim's Fur Mac and Spoon.

Naskapi Indians, Hare Krishna, Burger King.

Holland is more that 17 million selfies (or is it?).

Strolling Down Buffalo Memory Lane, with you, mon amour.

Schizophrenic means having religious ideas that we don't understand.

With or without youtube, but without (Vinyl Sounds Better Part 21 Grams).

Yahoo Parenting, Fantasy The Nice Remix Perfume and Rubber Soul Recovery.

Press here.

Out of focus.

Roger? Roger?

Flasher Player.

In Zipperspace.

Zen, chip, water.

Come Te Llamas.

Gone with the wind.

Language destroyed.

Change the way you play.

Pursuing virtual statehood.

To get with which program?

Love Is Falling On Us, folks!

And a kosher internet as well.

Riddled with bugs and back doors.

From gaming to droning to killing.

Collecting shells and bones, I remember.

Lone-wolf zealots and bison beta-bollocks.

Telecom firms thrive in Somalia despite war.

Grandmaster Flash & The Furious Jackson 5: Ben.

We must encourage the young to visit with the Elders.

Apple, Coca-Cola, Starbucks, Beats By Dre, Bank Of America.

A vibrant depiction of the creative power we have... ah, forget it!

Donny Trump, Gene Simmons, Hulk Hogan and other sex-media-giants.

Trump Triple: 3 oz. Smirnoff White Vodka, 2 oz. white spirit, ultimate white cream add-on.

Yes I would.

Eating out online.

'Cos we're Happy...

A World Under The Influence.

Donny Hathaway: The Ghetto.

Sorry, I'm just talking to my PC!

Explore the world, not the internet.

The privileged always make it home.

The Internet is NOT A Family Affair.

Big MacPhisto: Sundae Bloody Sundae.

An eye for an iPhone, a tooth for a Bluetooth.

Didn't I tell you your mind ain't no disc-drive?

Bono Christ & George W. Bush: V is for Venereal.

Like a Calvin Klein Jeans Infinite Indigo Candle in the wind.

Cut, copy, paste, match, waste, search, delete, destroy all files.

MacAirbnb, überpop, SushiSamba, Free Basics, Funk Formulas.

Barış Manço – Eğri Eğri Doğru Doğru (FOC Edits Rework, Remix).

Microsoft Oval Office 2018, Auto Wah Dada Funk and genital bass terror.

The Ronald McLaing Anti-Psychiatric Double Pounder HabsBurger works wonders!

David Beckham's H&M Bodywear Super Bowl Add and Paraphiliac Personality Disorder.

Mental illness is the result of being unable to cope with the way the world has been ordered.

New.

Be Stupid.

Lovely Day.

Deep world...

World Funk Rising.

This Doodle's Reach.

Hardware and Myth.

Doing without the rich.

Quick, fast, everywhere.

Religion and Photoshop.

No drinks in this toolbar.

Turning a page... delicious!

Cycling Down Lizard Lane.

Steve Jobscene wealth to thee!

Alice in WWWonderland NOT.

Virtuality leads to phantom pain.

Where Billy's bones are resting now.

The Self-Importance of Being Gates.

Software against ghosts and entities.

The Rolling Stones Official Mobile APP.

Sex from the time we did not have genitals.

Absolut Vodka is immanent and transcendent.

Hülya Süer – Şeker Oğlan (Kozmonot Rework).

The Bondage and Liberation of the Wifi People.

Minimize, zoom, bring all to front, all night long.

People with Googles Glasses shouldn't throw stones.

The world wide scope of demythologising our humanity.

Away away away away away away away away... finally away!

Protestant Thought before Andy Warhol's Campbell's Soap Pads, and after.

Uncle Ben Harper & The Innocent Criminals: The Crimes They're A'Changin'.

I would like to be a plush mandrill to be looked after by the girl of my choice: you!

M@m@.

Signing off.

Open Sores.

World Salat.

Special offer.

The Teardown.

Take your time.

You hit the spot.

Microsoft Records.

Who will set us free?

All software is Maya.

Nipple, Apple, bottle.

The Digerati of Doom.

Interact with lunatics.

Stupidity enjoys speed.

The Song Remains The Same.

Image Utility is hard to prove.

Superfast web and lion-bones.

Fast banking with slow money.

Forgetting to leave memory space.

I'm gonna wave my freak flag high!

The American Eagle Dance Nebula.

Killings shown online inspire more.

Cut Bill Gates at the knees of Reason.

Uncle Samsung Galaxy s6 Space War 3.

That a typewriter can sound like Mozart.

The Internet as oppressor of magic noise.

Like dolphins, we're better off swimming.

Where a woman rules, streams run uphill.

I'm having a real real-world problem here.

How video games fund arms manufacturers.

Anomalies and curiosities in digital medicine.

However near, the distance remains the same.

The rich are always complaining. ~ Zulu saying.

We're on the road to nowhere... come on inside.

Rock 'n roll/capitalist hybrids for the middle masses.

Inside Madonnald Trump's Unification Dollar Church.

What comes down is actually what rises within us, water.

Survivor military duty case + belt clip for iPod Touch & Kill.

The Crash of Comet Shoemaker-Levy-9 was a glamrock event.

Mad Madonna: La Isla Chiquita premium bananas (Just Smile Remix).

iBomber 3, Totem Destroyer Deluxe and National Prayer Breakfast live-stream.

I got a problem.

Microsoft Records.

Blacktronic Science.

Get loaded on Jesus!

Life in the Mac Zone.

Speaking in Tongues.

Searching for Zuckerberg.

Trapped Dead: Lockdown.

Garry Shider: Diaper Man.

Celebrity weightloss is here.

Fire-arms and video-games.

Curtis Mayfield: Move On Up.

Image Utility is hard to prove.

Burgers, fries and fast forward.

Buddy Holliday has left the internet.

And so we are back to Passports again!

Imarhan – Imarhan (Moscoman Remix).

Extremists, dissidents, knäckers, hackers.

The Rich Edit as opposed to the poor result.

A few fascists and a few hackers... life goes on.

The Virtual Kaleidoscope of Proletarian Celebrity.

A generation not being able to face real life situations.

Why is it we need to analyze and understand everything?

Corporate self-flattery and other techniques of advancing the world.

Pinokia.

Call of Duty.

No fun at all.

Yo Si Ti Ame.

See, Buy, Flee.

What the hack!

PCWorld's End.

Espionage is back!

Yelp! I Bing Somebody!

Wet T-Shirt Nite Online.

Imarhan – Assossamagh.

The Medusa Transducer.

Orion: Stellar Love Hurricane.

Uncle Samsung Galaxy s6 Space War 3.

Be MW: ConnectedDrive (DRIVE NOW!).

Isolation through gaming is very common.

My Creator, today I ask You to direct my thoughts.

The Brothers Johnson & Johnson: Clean and Clear.

GG All-in & Vodafone All-Stars: Back in the N.S.S.A.!

Cheb Khaled & Outlandish All-Stars: Aicha (Magreb Rework).

68% of church-going men view pornography on a regular basis.

Trump 2016 – By trying often, the monkey learns to jump from the tree.

Starstruck Colada: 2 oz. Alizé COCO, 2 oz. pineapple juice, 2 oz. nail polish remover.

Ooh Baby...

Too many images.

The New Selfabet.

Bee Gees: Tragedy.

I really have enough!

The Web Wide World.

What we shouldn't do.

Big McBang & Olufsen.

When I became fearful...

Stars, dots, stripes, coms.

Stranger in a strange land.

Here's looking at you, Bush.

Take it to the bridge too far!

PC Harvey: Down by the water.

What time is it in Arnhemland?

Preferring Altamira to Altavista.

Sharing the net, dividing the world.

No problem should be solved twice.

Harpooning for ancestral memories.

I don't have much money but boy if I did.

A kick in the balls of the Net if it had any.

One drawing a day keeps the doctor away.

Turn your wifi off at night, you sleep better.

Kentucky Freud Chicken comin' home to boast.

With a typewriter you know somebody is at home.

The good earth is rich and can provide for everyone.

In the digital age we'll see the end of... the digital age.

I order a record and you send me a pizza... what is this?

You always learn a lot more when you lose than when you win.

Malware, food guides, nutrition and diet tips from Jeb's own garden.

Etopia.

HP-Funk.

Just byte it.

Live Online.

Can you dig?

Unblock Me.

Simply clever.

In Fiberspace.

Inspire, expire.

Get busy 1 time.

We shall prevail.

Vanishing Point.

Devil's sidewalk.

Prove it all night.

Open your world.

Bring back the fax!

No stamp required.

Lost rivers to cross.

Disassembly Step 1.

Ants Across America.

Working for the rat-race.

Let your Palm be your Pilot.

Love in the black dimension.

The Not So Hidden Seducers.

To get lost is to learn the way.

A World Under The Influence.

Hell must be missing an angel.

Fixed ideas and mobile solutions.

Rise and shine and give God his glory!

Puzzler brain games for the unautistic.

Digital sea-salt is cocaine for believers.

Tweet Peaks (Fire Fox With Me Part 2).

Are you sure I haven't left my cable at...?

Digital playgrounds for robotic children.

Stay away from apocalyptic porn hybrids.

Small, medium, large, XL, XXL, XXX-Rated.

Jestofunk: Say It Again (Club MAD Remix).

Cheb Khaled N'ssi N'ssi Live In Casablanca.

Imagine – Version Speciale – Mami & Khaled.

Guilty protestants fear voodoo like nothing else.

A home for the homeless, a state for the stateless!

Secretary of State John Kurry beHeinz The Scenes.

Faster, smaller, slower, bigger, cheaper, rotten, fucked, free!

Mental graffiti for Internet Baboons and Stellar Help Desks for lonely wolves.

The Microsoft Snake Church Space Jazz Orchestra: St. Germain des Prés Live!

A 1000 years of virtuality, customers and Aztec skulls, The Noble Pinball Machine.

We want less!

The future is flat.

BT Tower Inferno.

Safety everywhere.

I can't read anymore.

Upgrade, downgrade.

Security versus privacy.

Like aerobics to sadhus.

Women prefer software.

A taste of the real America!

The Daily Horror of Celebs.

When a man loves a laptop.

Youtoogle the music charts.

I left my power cable in Ohio.

From language to non-language.

The privatisation of private parts.

Wicked are the ways of the world.

Circus of Money, Psychosis Beach.

Rachid Taha – Ecoute moi camarade.

Solved problems aren't of any use to us.

Copy and print, kiss and fly, buy and die.

The Semi-Erotic Cornflakes Funfair Affair.

We were the change we had been waiting for.

They have a name for all the winners in the world.

7 hits of Coca Cola makes you drink 1 orange juice.

Wealth, if you use it, comes to an end; learning, if you use it, increases.

Zoom.

Unroll Me.

Eyes wasted.

Loose to win.

Machine Hell.

Down with IT.

Drop The Box.

And you are?...

Blah blah blah.

Need for speed.

Stop this world.

What is an icon?

Vogue Anorexia.

Just try drawing.

Numb to cruelty.

Angels don't surf.

Enter The Future.

We had IT coming.

American Backslide.

Cyber guns are guns.

Depraved and wired.

Pleasure is elsewhere.

Check my order status.

Spreading the message.
Microsoft World Order.
Verbal pleasure is down.
Ted & Tom, Cruizzifried.
And DOS created woman.
Do more with your phone.
From reptile to bird to PC.
Wishbones for e-business.
Tap to install world-peace.
The Internet has no bones.
Get in the know in no time.
Do Da Da Ball Street Shuffle.
From one second to the next.
It takes a village to raise a child.
A 1000 names for nothing at all.
Public toilets for private creeps.
Lampedusa is not virtual reality.
There's no Internet in Dreamtime.
The Great Denial (Clear History II).
Stay informed. Be inspired. Get out.
Apparently the sun is out of fashion.
In a perfect, Apple Authorized world.
Cosmic names for commercial goods.
Docking my black boat in a video port.
Robots all over me, let me die in peace.
Drooling over my mouse and keyboard.
Money Minute: 5 signs you're too cheap.
The Times we live in are not on our side.
Ronald MacDonald Airdrop the bombast!
Built to make you an unstoppable asshole.
The TomTom Club: Under The Boardwalk.
The current application will be terminated.
How Wall Street may threaten your pension.
Leave me alone, sell me nothing, robots in my brain.
Rock 'n roll capitalist hybrids for the middle masses.
Living in the age of populism on the rise world-wide.
Rachid Taha – Ya Rayah (Clip Officiel, HD, Rai, Pop).
Charlize Theron doesn't want women to be afraid of aging.
Bruce Webber & November 8th 2016 All-Stars: Broken Noses.

I can breathe underwater, I can walk through walls, I can swim in fire.

Mad Mix: Gordon's Gin, Campbell Soup, Red Bull, liquid Risperdal, lighter fluid.

FB (I).

Skip All.

Save ass.

Leave a note.

Read my loops.

The largest ever.

Of Mice and Men.

Electric honey doesn't flow.

Computers don't make sense.

Born this way, gone the other.

Force feedback and spirit visions.

Doctor, doctor, I have a malware infection.

Millions of records in a fraction of seconds.

David Beckham Classic: Revise Your Classics.

You don't really want to do it but you do it anyway.

Look deep into nature, and you will better understand.

Smash Pin Rage, e-spot cyclones and Adobe Privacy Settings.

Your entire creative world, now in one place, completely ruined.

Finding truth.

Search the store.

All rights reserved.

iPhone 6 and the City.

Zombie Virus Survival.

Blackberry fields forever.

PlainTalk is software for liars.

The Motherboard Connection.

Flamingoes and flash-memory.

Maggot Brain: The Video Game.

Sergei Eisenstein preferred film.

In a cinema, you can feel warm and safe.

The Online Aboriginal Healthy Food Guide.

Local neurosis comes with global psychosis.

This Is A Call: The Life and Times of Dave Grohl.

With Busta Rhymes in the Drive-Thru of Americana.

Talkshows destroy our language, as does the computer.

When my mom's robot comes into my room to give me a goodnight kiss.

Citizen Ex.

#Op Tunesia.

I'm an animal.

I refuse to smile.

Never Hott Enuff.

The Best of Debussy.

I've been watching you.

It's all about the money.

Out-computing the enemy.

Verification and Validation.

I just got out of the Internet!

Coming out the shadows of e.

Sly & The Family Stone: LIFE!

The Holy River will hold us all.

Steely Stanford: Harvard Moon.

Into the Silicon Valley of Darkness.

Punctuality is the virtue of the bored.

e-smoke signals and nanotechnology.

Les murs de poussières nous attendent.

I revolucanise by my eructions, Armorica.

Que Sarah Sarah (Whatever Bill Be Bill Be).

Your algorithmic liability is questionable, Sir.

Time flies over us, but leaves its shadow behind.

Before you go virtual, make a good arthouse film.

The poor and ignorant, they mostly die, eaten by e.

Ego, Super Ego, ID, passport, password, Wifi Cody.

Dr. Phil ft. Bootsy Collins: Something in the air that night.

3D Touch. Photos 12 Mpx. Videos 4k. Un seul mot: puissance.

The unwanted are unwanted because that's what they are: unwanted.

Uncle RAM, Colonel Gaddaft Punk & Digital Disco-Nepotist All Stars: Get Lucky.

Online distribution can be brought on by winds, currents and similar natural forces.

Pop-up-tv, pop-up-art, pop-up-musea, pop-up-koons, pop-up-culture, pop-up-pop-up...

Simon Posthuma & A Fool Such As I No Corrida All-Stars: Footnotes On The Dancefloor.

Trolling Down: The art of deliberately and openly pissing people off via internet terminology.

ZAPP!

AutoFill?

Accept Cookies!

Data make us lonely.

On Safetyfirst Street.

Revolution in the head.

Pomme, Pomme, Pomme.

For whole the world to see.

Here, there and everywhere.

Hotdog, MacBook, meatball.

iPhone SE. Petite Révolution.

A flower doesn't smell online.

Riverrun, past atoms and bits...

Creating illnesses and appetites.

Apple Watch. Du. Auf Einen Blick.

Introducing... Macbook Proletariat.

There's a war going on in our sexuality.

Billy 'Idol' Gates: Dancing With Myself.

Into the Dark Valley of Siliconsumption.

I must govern the clock, not be governed by it.

Everybody video taping everybody all the time.

The winds of love will blow off the shades of night.

Die Apple Watch überwacht meine Herzfrequenz!

Time is what we want most, but what we use worst.

Hillary is a monologue about Monologue Lewinsky.

Onlineness is creating a global, collective psychosis.

James Marshall McLuhan: All Along The Watchtower.

Startup: The Mecca Mouse & Gaufi Arabian Dizney World War.

The Australian French Language Class Part 1: Oui Madame, moi Ozzy.

What's all the excitement about these hi-tech pocket calculators anyway?

Johnny Sitar Watson: A Real Mother For Ya (Mother Theresa Dub Remix).

My TomTom navigator told me to make a U-turn and I crashed into the Anti-Christ.

Drowning in a Pina-Cola-Colada in the Church of The Scientology Celebrity Centre.

Ignore it.

Sell your debt.

Other People Think.

Question d'Equilibre.

Every click you make.

Bush is a demonologue.

Into the glory of the Light.

Not Dead Yet (Phil Collins).

Over and out, ask your soul.

Brother, can you spare a dime?

As long as the grass shall grow.

Thank God Love Lives Forever.

Let's go down to the Holy River.

Is this you? (This is not really me).

A little something funky to blow your socks off.

News is what someone somewhere decides it is.

On the Seneca reservation there is much sadness now.

Agora, Second Life and Shell Easy Clear cockpit wipes.

This program is available until March 30th 2028 23.58.

A Win-Windows situation for Bill Gutzappuffalo HillBilly Graham.

Microsoft Office Erotics and celebrity perfumes discouraged by Malcolm X.

Anyway, all these computers and digital gadgets are no good (Prince 1958-2016).

John Lennon, Simon Posthuma & Graham Nashville Fight Night: Fresh Out Of Hell Part 2.

People who cannot find time for recreation are obliged sooner or later to find time for illness.

Low as Linux.

In the Coke Zone.

I liked our postman.

Peerless, wireless, homeless.

Digital feng shui is awesome.

Resting on the shoulders of giants.

Medicine: your money and your life.

Steve Jobs: San Francisco of Assissi.

That it's nobler to suffer in the mind.

The Revenant always returns to bass.

Women, madness and computer culture.

Time is flying never to return until it does.

Wreckless Eric Schmidt: Whole Wide World.

Wreckless Eric Schmidt 2: A Roomful of Monkeys.

The earth became mobile after man conquered the Cloud.

Pure madness goes hand in hand with global connectivity.

Privacy, freedom, control, security, buddhism, compassion.

All the world's information in the palm of your hand... Christ!

'The internet's completely over' (Prince Roger Nelson 1958-2016).

The only reason for time is so that everything doesn't happen at once.

Smiley Cyrus & The Emoticon All-Starlets: Creamy beaver hotter than a fever.

It is high time that children explained to their parents the mystery of sexual life.

Encryption of Life.

God's Own Microsoft.

Your kids are spoiled?

Google vs. Bangladesh.

Rationality = Superstition.

e-cummerce, e-commerde.

Colouring the humain brain.

Too much agreement kills a chat.

Not Dead Yet... (George H. Bush).

Sarah 'Soupline' Palin: Glisse Parfaite.

AXIOMERICA: Shankar | Soul Searcher.

Jesus Christo Silicon Valley Curtain 1970.

Soon everyone on Earth will be connected.

The medium, the massage and the deception.

Spotlight search in the Digital Age of Darkness.

A monkey can type out the work of Paul Auster.

Google is a monologue about world domination.

Water is the memory of the world, fire the consumer.

Future connectivity and revolution by consciousness.

Reshaping the future of People, Nations and Businesses.

The Internet is a standing invitation to a mental beheading.

We gathered here today to get through this thing called Life.

Hide nothing, for time, which sees all and hears all, exposes all.

Boozing my way into Oblivion at the base of the economic pyramid.

In the American Church of Scientechnology only a few are welcome.

iRobot's Roomba, schizo-voice recognition and Heinz Driver's Seatz.

Twitter: Riding the massive swell of reporting, information and global gossip.

Future connectivity promises a dazzling array of quality of life improvements.

Ronaldo McDonaldo, Zizango 'Mango' Zidango & The Réal Clones of Francostein.

A source of potentially dreadful evil but for sure: full-blown, transparent mediocrity.

Pseudo linguistics, commercial drone warfare, Lonely iPatty Hearst Club Bandwidth.

Picture Youtube Imperialism? The impact of US Television and Internet in Latin America.

Hooked up.

Hunger PC.

Cold as Coldplay.

Oui c'est mon Mac!

My lover's dropbox.

Tu. A colpo d'occhio.

This is What You Get.

Bankrupt emotionally.

Terminology = Ideology.

Thermo Nuclear Twitter.

Bring Back My Happiness.

Anxiety: Taste The Feeling.

The Spitting Dadalai Lama.

e-crime, cause and solution.

Sync your soul to your iPhone!

RHCP: Stadium PayPalladium.

So unelegant! So unintelligent!

Spreading e across the nations.

D'ya belong to the bandwidth poor?

How to print your constant worries.

'Undeniable depth.' Financial Times.

Protect yourself from what you want.

Silicon Valley: White Punks On Dope.

BlackBerry White: Rhapsody in White.

I want to talk about it: Colonized Minds.

Uncle Jamiroquai: Little L. Ron Hubbard.

Heinz Dreamz and milkshake phantasy life.

Below the ocean instant sperm alpha waves.

From the nipple to the Apple never satisfied.

www and the physical nature of the Universe.

Popfuscation outside the electronic paper trail.

An ounce of prevention is worth a pound of cure.

Download a future full of isolation, girls and boys.

Kidicool Care & Cacao Coala Bearsatz child labor.

Paris Hilton Hotel Californication – en savoir plus.

Billy 'Idol' Gates and the Digital Meatball Controversy.

iPhone Plus there's no way they're getting away with this.

The option to delete (near-permanent) data is an illusion.

iWork That Body Shopping species to the ground of Unreason.

The raping of Mother Earth by the multinationals of yesterday.

Microsoft Office Erotics for Mac 2016 Home & Business Edition.

Government, surveillance, control, security, Kellogg's Fruit Loops.

Que Sarah Sarah: John McCain Homefrit Security – huile de tournesol.

Microsoft World Peace and the Internet Glaucoma Bliss-consciousness.

Agenda 23, Paleo WIPP Express and narcissistic personality désordoridant.

Fighting against secrecy that shields actions not in the interest of the public.

Paris Hilton John, Elisabeth Taylor Swift, Louis Ferdinand Paul Céline Dion.

U See A Rock On The Shore And Say It Has Always Been There, And Will Stay There.

Sai Mohammad Ali Baba Cool & the neurolinguistic correction of digital speech defects.

Get social!

Dionys.o.s.

1 YEAR FREE.

About This Mac.

Planet Google Earth.

Auto Save Our Souls!

Get smart with media.

Become a gesture guru.

The Monolinguistics of e.

Recent items, past dreams.

Empty trash, empty kitsch.

FaceTime, voodoo and iChat.

Boost your productivity today!

Your needs, and only your needs.

Digital drunks and iToolbarflies.

Into the garden of Earthly Elites.

Eat, Sleep, Restart and Shutdown.

Web wonders and worldly catastrophes.

This is your Mac's defunct web browser.

Free your disk and your drive will follow.

Secure your afterlife today. Inscribe now!

AXIOMERICA: Nicky Skopelitis: Ekstasis.

Running Win-Windows on a Wacko Macko.

Time is the most valuable thing a man can spend.

Microsoft Gold Certified Assholes, official partner.

Let's start the War On Tourism, peoples of this earth!

Applying for honey at the Billy & Lizzy Gucci Foundation.

Get to grips with Pages, burgers, bytes, Trump and Inhalin' Palin.

Step into the world of the Grand Funk Apple Mac Disorder Circus.

I, me, myself, Mac mini-skirts and iPenis-protexplosive dust jackets.

Manage your login items, bison hides and Shell EasyClean screen wipes.

Online Grand Funk Canyon Cave-Art and PPPOPS access to the Universe.

Bill Lasworrell & The Hallucination Engine Interfunk Bass Brigade: Stomp!

Rewriting Warhol: Electric Cheerleader 11 times in Google (Triple Disaster).

Paris Hilton ft. The Holiday Inn Hotaliban All-Stars: Hit your bodies to the floor.

Baracksz Husseinz Beanz Laden: Obamma Got Osamma (Club Navy Seal Remix).

Jamais.

I will follow...

Beat it! Beat it!

Winter Is Coming.

50 shades of trash.

What's your budget?

Who created the @-Bomb?

The End of the sPC's is nigh.

The Quick Renaming of Paradise.

Follow us on the edge of darkness.

He comes from a good home movie.

All Move To Trash and stay trashed.

Key Infoaming at the mouth of Reason.

Apps, games, drones, gadgets, microwaves.

Captain John Beefheartfield: America Dada.

One moment please.... your card is being checked.

20 fantastic ways to personalise your Wacko Macko.

If you don't know who you are, look at where you come from.

The Holiday-In-The-Sun MacDrive-Inn Zuckerburger Manual.

Snapshooting e-mails into the Vanilla Sky of e-Scienzayatollalia.

Smart groups, smart albums, smart folders, smart playlists, smart mailboxes.

Get organized.

Eros and Light.

Cash at first sight.

Let's funk... let's roll...

The world's not sharing.

Forgotten, passed worlds.

The world is vintage today.

Smile... You're in Matongé!

DigiDutchland Unter Alles.

In the rumbling waters of e.

Real pleasure is never guilty.

Doin' the ol' Jujutube Magic.

BASE: Welcome To Freedom.

The e-Voyage of the Voodoo Gods.

e, Time, Creation and the Continuum.

Do more with your Mac, like eating out.

Public wireless hot spots, like Barbara Bush.

We are naked like the sharp eye of the lizard.

Prick up your Mac and loosen your talktapes.

Zuckerbourgeois down to his teeth and bones.

The L. Ronald MacDonald Hubbard Telescope.

Google mixed with salty foam and love refound.

Get the full download of unworldly bollocks here.

When the Ship of Oblivion sets sail on the e-ocean.

Ahh, the worldwideweb, I'd really wish it didn't exist.

AirBNP Paribas Fortis: The bank for a changing world.

www: Do Not Board | Ne Pas Embarquer | Nicht Aufsteigen.

Sarah Palin's High Tea Party: John McCain mini croquettes – extra croustillant.

Freedom really comes into play the moment you start doing something interesting with it.

So Lonely.

Miles Ahead.

Think Stereo!

See what's new.

Please Give Now.

Microsoft Sword.

iPhone ti aspetta.

Can all this be true?

Doom With A View.

A joystick is forever.

Nightmares do pass.

Get isolated for free!

Suggested favorites...

The Prodigy: Firestarter.

The World's Bending Will.

The Menu Bar is open now.

Force Quit your job if you can.

Ti tiene in forma. A tutti livelli.

Mars is the skull of the warrior.

WhiteBerry Black: Sho' You Right.

Digital Disclosures of the 3rd Kind.

Living in the age of Internextuality.

iPhones, moules, frites et crevettes.

We'll call the winds and the end of e.

Ego Planet – Nettoyant multi-surface.

Hugo BALLSDSM-5 | Supersoulfighter.

Connectivity rises faster than our oceans.

Like a bird in flight – a hieroglyph of Truth.

I do take salt on my fish 'n processor chips.

How to control who does what on your Mac.

Billy 'Gucci' Graham Central Stationtostation.

Mc: American McMorning, African McMorning.

Like Me! (Bet Cha You Say That To All The Girls).

Misery is not my friend, I'll break free before I bend.

Let's go and see the stars, the Milky Way and even Mars.

More Mc: Amazing Angus Young, Generous Jack White.

Bill Gates ALS Ice Bucket Challenge MUST SEE VIDEO.

Murky Mirk Sucxerberg, the King of Candy, Matongé, BXL.

Low-cost information, low-grade reporting, low-life gossip.

Hillary Clinton, a good show starts in the dressing room ya!

Bienvenue chez Paris Hilton Hotels, HHonours and Resorts.

Funk Shui: The winds of change passing through our genitals.

iChat, FireFox, Cyberduck, Thunderbird, No iDogs 'n Irishmen.

e, rain, water, waterfall of chance, we are naked, Naked in the Rain.

Growing electric pineapples on Mars is a typically paranoid vision.

Custom transfers unleash your personality with Plus F* off big time and forever.

Tasty Rocky Mountains: 3⅓ oz. Van Gogh BLUE Vodka, sour mix, magnesium peroxide.

Mohammayaan Hirsi Ali Baba & The 40 Neo-Con Thieves of the World: Bush, Rove, Rice etc.

McChina.

Pricy Part 3.

Another life.

Protect & Care.

Total 0% Petrol.

Imperial Vanilla.

www and the Absolute.

A replacement for sleep?

Children working overtime.

Life, Internet and Non-Life.

Got 2B or Not 2B Styling Gel.

imPêche Bush 88.5% alcohol.

Make Africa Great Again 2020.

And make @ name for yourself!

Animals are naked, don't forget.

www et la Permanence du Stoïcisme.

Bill Gates Barbecue & Grill Degreaser.

iPhone 6-packs and iNivea douchebags.

The virtual memory of earthly experiences.

Rock Gel, Rasta Paste & Fluo Bluetooth-aches.

When you click cancel to get rid of the world you live in.

Jumping naked into the fire, just like a true bison would.

Our largest, untapped natural resource: Human Potential.

The Cloud: Cirrus, Cumulus, Cirrocumulus, Cumulonimbus.

Bootsy Collins' thumbprints and Paleo Indian animals tracks.

Get started with iNivea Hawaii Flower & Oil of Olazzmatrazz.

iMaster beats by Jeb Bush (Last Night The DJ Saved His Wife).

Microsoft OSX, Flint Axiom Records and Apache Rose Peacock.

Microsoft Excel 2058 and Paleo Power Point-read-only space poetry.

Funky Munch: Sir Psycho that is me, sometimes I feel the need to scream.

MacPuke Pro, Dr. Oetker Ibizza Tradizionale and online Bref Powder Encounters.

Davy Lynch & Trancendental Meditation Jazzmatrash Orchestra: Do It For Van Gogh!

Be Breezer – a refreshing blend of oxblood, battery acid, Bacardi Rhum and fruit flavours.

Itzzz Pay Day Pal!

The iPhone X-Ray.

Like-ty split go snap snap.

My dentist told me I have Blueteeth.

You're so prepaid, my lovely usherette!

Obama's Secret Drone Wars: PTSD-DAY 1.

Monotony is a monologue about a monologue,

Globalisation anxiety seeps into everyday lives.

An introduction to the metaphysics of Billy Goats.

Zen buddhist meditation in data-rich environments.

In the Hanging Octopussy's Garden of Nerdly Delights.

Lunatics on pogo sticks, another Southern fried freak on a cruxifix.

Earth, www, troposphere, stratosphere, mesosphere, thermosphere, exosphere.

Republicans are a monologue about Democrats are a monologue about Republicans.

Microsoft Excess for Mac is the rightful match to its applauded Wim Wenders cousin.

Watermelon Freedom: 1 oz. Tito's Handmade Vodka, watermelon juice, 2 oz. ammonium.

The digital bureaucratic doublespeak of the likes of Jobs, Cook, Gates, Schmidt, Zuckerberg.

Sarah Palin & The Alaska Human Potential Movement: McCocain running around her brain.

Pop Life.

Skin I'm In!

I Agree (Not).

Be indifferent.

Privacy Revisited.

The Whistle of Bloz.

Oops... Easy Access!

e, Sense et Non-Sense.

Switch the view indeed.

Can we find a reason why?

Walking on the moon of e.

Be wash (in the wash to be).

Prozac is a destructive force.

Where wild wherewolves live.

America is a tragedy of errors.

Our infinite need for Oblivion.

Show Room With A View options.

HH/MMA Internet Demolition Ltd.

Data we process when you use Google.

Light will be shed on the darkness of e.

A good alternative for brains is silence.

Plan of White Thoughts I see in the Valley.

Des impressions qui font forte impression.

Do more with your Mac, like nightclubbing.

Hamburgers, computers and school shootings.

Super Soul! Super Soul! Super Soul that is coming!

Place your microchips in the bottom of a highball glass.

USA and other L. Ronald MacDonald Trumpadelic nonsense.

Tony Blair is a Catholic monologue about his own historical guilt.

Inside the digital underground and the battle of our connected world.

Let's forget, you and me, let's forget the world and all that comes with it.

George Clinton & The On-Nile All That Jazzigators: Paint Trump's White Ass Black.

Get Off.

Enjoy Time.

Microsoft Cowboy.

In a hurry, for what?

The iCeman.Cometh.

Lady iChatterley's Lover.

Just like you always have.

Einstürzende iNeubauten.

Increase your profitability.

Feed your visual addiction.

Making Life simple... right!

This precious world of ours.

Schizophrenia doesn't exist.

RAM, REM & The Rat Man.

Under the cherry moon of e.

Creativity and daydreaming.

Answer your creative calling.

Staring at I don't know what.

Virtue in the Cave of Reason.

Shyness, withdrawal, browsing.

Webcamming and netcumming.

PC Harvey: The Orange Monkey.

Glued to the screen of deception.

Tetsumi Kudo is my pilot, peoples.

It's all about time, it's all about love.

Let's talk about verbal virtuality first.

Time is sensuality, not loss of money.

I Never Promised You A Prose Garden.

On the talent crisis in the digital realm.

The Internet is an endless hall of mirrors.

Conqueror 2Neutral says who you are too.

Plastic Bertrand Cantat: Ça plane pour moi.

When your time really should be your money.

Capture the image as you see it when you see it.

Youtube and the phantasy life of blind children.

Introducing the Live-Stream of Consciousness.

Guoyu, English, Great Russian, Spanish, Google.

On a computer screen everything looks the same.

Von Monet Zu Jeff Koons (and happily back again).

Sony ∝350: Your only limitation is your imagination.

Gestalt therapy, online television viewing and aggression.

Microsoft Mon Homère, the iLiad & the 2016 eSpace Odyssey.

Daydreaming of Paris in the Hilton Hotel of Severe Memory Loss.

Brian Geiser & The iPatti Smith Groupsex All-Stars: Dancing barefoot.

Subscribe to continuous creativity or buy carefree Pay-as-you-go credits.

Sgt. Cessna's Lonely Hearts Auto Club Band: Do You Know Thee Enemy?

Billy Watergates, Keith Richard Nixons & The Scrolling Stones: Hey Negrita!

The Child's World of Make-Believe: Experimental studies in Imaginative play.

Call Carlos Slim Cessna: Three Bloodhounds Two Shepherds One Fila Brasileiro.

Purple Brain hemisphere dominance and electrical activity of green anteaters online.

Gun smoke, Paleo wish fullfilment and achievement motivation of unsatisfied people.

E-ROPA.

Coming to be...

RAMBrandt's Eyes.

Irrationality is a great good.

Every need got an ego to feed.

www.platomisosoupism.com.

Greek thought, Google culture.

ACNN/DCNN: Highway To Hell.

The Logos of the Living Online World.

I'm the slime in your video conference.

On the Dotcommon Sense of the World.

A treatise on Google as the first principle.

We somehow all live in Connecticut today.

Gilbert & Gordon's Social e-Gin Sculpture.

On the mystical shape of the Google godhead.

The New World Gnomeland Security Project.

I'm the tool of the Government and the Industry too.

PC Harvey: The Hope iPhone Six Demolition Project.

The human brain is not ready for all this, it really isn't.

Ali Chemicali & The DSM-5 Big Band: Pharmazooropa (full album).

Mc Mick Joggerwacky, Jerry Halliburton & The Rolling Stone Ice Age 3: Satisfaction.

Home!

Accedi.

Wikilooks.

Get it now!

Prince-Art.

All Night Long.

Remember me.

Sjef Van Google.

Their lost youth.

Give All To Love.

Breakfast Can Wait.

Black Budget Friday.

Whistle tha' tha' limit?

The electrolysis of love.

About Proximus | Fonk!

Plan of the Google Cave.

Steely Spam: Dirty iWork.

Next time connect for free.

When Google Met Tipilooks.

When men first began to play.

Google+ F* Off Big This Time!

Internutters and webbastards.

Redeeming my promosexuality.

Man clad in the glory of the Bill.

Connectivity Benefitz Terroristz.

Heidi Cruz: Chico Chico Charlie.

A Purple Reign – a documentary.

Z: Hey Hey We're Glad To Be Jay.

The Better Nature of Our Angels.

Bison burgers and Google shakes.

On the notion of the Supervirtual.

Prince: Cave-Art Official Stone Age.

Aaaahhh... Lovely Rutte – meter maid.

Trading in primal arts is wrong as well.

iTunafish no swim in no ocean of mine.

Upon the Burning of our House of Love.

Like a moth to the flame burnt by the wire.

The winternet is lurking within my moods.

Your computer may be at risk, like yourself.

DSM-5-UB40-XXXL: The Burden Of Shame.

Roland Clark presents Digital Pimps: The Sun.

DJ Afrojerk & The White House Music Program.

McZuckerburgers lead to Obezos across the nations.

The Electric Spanking of Trillion Dollar War Babies.

DJ (Stormin') Norman Van Buuren: The Bolero Briefings.

The Silvergreen Ants of Online Seduction: Bring them on!

I just printed my McChicken Voodoo Nuggets in full colour.

Do I not loathe Apple walls, Google streets, Microsoft stones?

Poor-to-poor file-sharing and difficult-to-trace-virtual-currency.

Disembowelled bison, prostrate nerd and joystick topped by a bird.

Direct fan mail to Prince, P.O. Box 4475, North Hollywood, CA 91607.

Iraq – Telecoms, Mobile, Broadband and Kentucky Fried Dating-sites.

The world's first drone-based no-fly zone will probably also be the last.

Da Bootsy & Da Bush: The Wuthering Heights of the Bootzillacon Valley.

And the song, from beginning to end, I found again in the heart of a friend.

Reverend Moon & The Linda 'Luv' Goodman Sun Sign Singers: Cosmic Girl.

Choose Proximusic Internet and access all our Brian Ferry hotspots for free.

Shakin' Jay Zuckerberg, Steven 'Tyler' Hawking & Bio-Beyoncécémel Hérosmith: B&W.

'Microsoft Mon Amour is both profoundly readable and wondrously wise'. Walter Isaacson.

My liver exploded from online pollution, on my way to the top of the Internet Mountain.

I like my new telephone, my computer works just fine, but Lord, I miss my mind!

The production of too many useful things results in too many useless people.

Do you realise if it weren't for Edison we'd be watching TV by candlelight?

If it keeps up, man will atrophy all his limbs but the push-button finger.

The knack of so arranging the world we don't have to experience it.

Tony Berlusconi & The Maffia Macaroni: Se bastasse una canzone.

Warning: the Internet may contain traces of nuts.

Hooked on Internet? Help is a just a click away.

Bill says I'm the one but the kid is not my son.

The Internet is the trailer park for the soul.

You can set your Apple watch by it.

The 21st Century Steam Machine.

Grist to the 3rd millennium.

Blue screen of death.

Switch to: me!

DSMTV-5.

Pez Pez Pez.

On Racebook.

Burma online.

Lascaux Crazy!

No Place To Hide.

La Vie Est Violente.

These Days Are Mine.

Here IT Comes Again.

Digital waterboarding.

Nerd: Run To The Sun.

Thine Eyes Still Shined.

We are mates in misery.

Are U Gonna Go myWay?

Capsizing in the ocean of e.

Love in the blue dimension.

Happy XXX-Mass America!

Don't Shoot The Messenger.

Taking u down, and up again.

In Him We Live (Steve Jobs).

Next to of course God america i.

Why don't you get back into bed?

The only Bush I know is Kate Bush.

Rest In Peace Philip Seymour Hoffman.

Though all the fates should prove unkind.

And the virtual world's version of the world.

Wearable technology, unbearable technology.

The Crazy Things Ted Cruz Actually Believes In.

House of Black Lanters feat. Gitmozoid: Broken.

In pathless paths online, I lead my wandering feet.

Trafficking in bulk leaks in order to change the word.

Jelly Belly Gates & The New York Peppermint iPatties.

The Skype Report – A study in human online sexuality.

Doin' Da Jujutubular Bellsex Magick in Zauberspace Out!

And you may ask yourself: where is that large automobile?

BlackBerry Gibb & The Digital 21+ Busy Beegees: Stayin' Alive.

You can walk a mile in my shoes but you can't dance a step in my feet.

King Edward Snowden III: Truth is coming, and it can not be stopped.

Emir Kusturica & The Balkanisation of the Internet: Unza Unza Time.

All smartphones are equipped with some form of poor-to-poor capability.

Vinny Verax, information transparency and more slurred Pentagon speech.

Brillo, Auto Da Funk and VoIPPP2PPP networking societies the world over.

High quality 3D models of people to be compressed and transmitted anywhere.

Henry 'The Horse' Kissinger & White Heroin House Party People: Crazy Horses 2.

Mike 'Strawberry' Oldfields Forever & Youtubular Bells Big Band: What's Ya Flava?

'Microsoft Mon Amour is a brilliant guidebook for the 21st century'. Richard Branson.

Carlos 'The Jackall' Slim Cessna Grand Theft Auto Club Crazy: Crazy (Navy Seal Mix).

Badge of Honor: 1 oz. Pucker Lemonade Lust Vodka, 3 oz. Club Soda, ½ oz. sulphuric acid.

Schizo-voice-over-Internet-protocol and the insertion of bits into the origin of the world.

See also.

Free gmail.

Google Minus.

Planet Cocktail.

Coldplaystation.

Frequently used.

The Big Lewinsky.

Do As De La Does.

Bones For Beginners.

Only Lovers Left Alive.

If I was your girlfriend.

Standing by a parking meter...

The men of Lascaux were rich.

Doth Comb her velvet Capitall.

Trump est un gros dégueulasse.

The cosmological inflation of e.

Camp's Critique of Pure Reason.

Hacking: the act of stealing jokes.

How is your Würm, Mr. Branson?

I'm a puncushion, and that's a fact.

Live From Mars: Ben Harper is a reality.

Ah Ah Ah Ah Stayin' Alive, Stayin' Alive...

Brian 'McMick' Ferry: She's The Hugo Boss.

Barackless Eric transschmidting Live from Mars.

Scritti Grafitti BXL: L'amour est mort en Amérique.

Sun and moon and day and night and Bill and beast.

Where tigers talk to bisons, turtles are the translators.

The Internet is a cluster not of everything but of anything.

Deleting freedom: The David Icke Pricke Videocast Trailer.

There's a dark cloud of information growing over our heads.

We Want More: Google Plus Plus Plus Plus Plus Plus Plus.

Billy G.: His Glorious Handywork not made by his own two hands.

Rewriting De La Warhol: Ecce Omo Soap Pads (A Little Bit Of Soap).

Zero Palin & Kurt McCain T-Party People: Smells Like Teenage Spirit.

Janis Chopin & The Mirror Palace of Cheap Thrills: Me and Billy McGeetes.

Microsoft Ultra Doux Shampooing au lait digital hydratant (Cheveux normaux).

Friedrich 'Dritte Walt' Disneytsche & The Runduckfunk Radio-Stars: Ich Glotz TV.

Yahooped.

Lonely days.

In Spacebook.

Bonzzzzzzzzzzour!

I wanna be your lover.

Product (RED) BULL.

The Ohio Players: Wire!

Love sexy, down by the river.

Ego, Super Ego & 3rd Eye(l)Id.

Repairing dead pigeons online.

Worms Against Nuclear Killers.

One Mann Show: Der Cyberberg.

What has gone wrong with the world?

Beyoncé: biodegradable et compostable.

When billions of more people cum online.

Franco Goes To Hollywood (Franco GTH).

If you can't win the game, change the rules.

Nerds, worms, humans, viruses, cockroaches.

On the Internet all amounts to the same old song.

... the titanic centralising evil they are constructing...

You Can't Read This Book: Censorship in the Age of Freedom.

Nerds, Twizzlers, Jawbreakers, Necco wafers, Jolly Ranchers.

Got the bill and Rutte paid it (Took her home I nearly made it).

www is a commercial battle with profound security implications.

Twin Bison Testicles and off-the-shelf facial-recognition software.

Google Books today does not rate intellectual property rights very highly.

Sly & The Prince-Art Official Family Stone Age: It' A Funknroll Family Affair.

Cyber-attack capability and New Code Warbabies Makin' New Code Warbabies.

'Microsoft Mon Amour is a book that defines the nature of the new world'. Tony Blair.

Communicating and intercoursing with remote users as natural as face-to-face exchange.

One Lapdog Per Child.

When Black Friday comes.

The FireWall Street Journal.

They can hack all but my heart.

Google Plussycat faster kill kill!

When by the digital Ruins oft I past.

The e-River Swelleth More and More.

Evolution contemporarily out of order.

Billy 'Purple' Hague: Toryhallastoopid.

Grand Identity Theft Auto Da Fee Club Meat.

MAD, NASA, MILNET, US NAVY, BARBAPAPA.

Milk Duds, Pixie Stix, Candy Corn, Gummi worms.

Sustainability: The 2009 Green Revolution in Iran.

The Ambrosia of the Google God's a Weed on Earth.

John Major Tom Cruz Control: Zigital Stardust Memories.

Prince & Art Official 3rd Eye Family Stone Age: P-Funknroll.

Know It All, Exploit It All, Collect It All, Process It All, Forget It All.

Franco GTH: L'Oréal Madrid Indestructible KVH 96H Extreme Style.

Through our colonized mind we will ultimately find the gateway to freedom.

Keith Alexanderichards & the Five 3rd Eyes Intelligence Alliance: Hey Negrita 2!

Jared Cohen & The Paleo Policy Planning Staff Members: iCondoleeza Rice Pops!

When are you free to take some tea with me (Lovely Rutte, meter maid, ah) Rutte!

The Net has been transformed into the most dangerous facilitator of totalitarianism.

Tony TRAX, Mary MENDAX, Peter PrimeSuspect & The Brides of Wikistein: Stomp!.

A Brief History of Slime.

In the country of last things.

The Net, the Flesh and the Spirit.

In the iClinique of Mental Reduction.

@tomic Fireball and Bifi Wifi 3x Roll pops.

Microsoft Symphonie Nr. 777 in dsm-moll 5.

Here and now and yesterday all is in the past.

Dancing With Wolfgang Amantonin Mozartaud.

Flyin' High: Middle Aurignacian Economy Class.

The New Digital H and other Sir Nose Job rituals.

Apocalyptica, Goo Google Dolls, VD1 Rock Honors.

There will not be peace between nerds and animals.

e.e. cummings: a man who had fallen among thieves.

Apple: don't let them fool ya, or even try to school ya.

Within the electronic brain circuit of this plodding life.

The sound of a typewriter is music to the ears of Psyche.

LSDélicieux: 60 recettes Républicaines à base d'insectes.

By the way, tell Sir Mick, black girls want to be loved all day.

Microsofty, LSDSM-Chanel No. 5, Sir Bob + Bobette Geldof.

Dave Icke Pricke 1: Agenda 21 – Blueprint For Global Control.

Soul travels in the Encryptorium and the invention of solitude.

e-hova witnesses, angelic online help and file-driver protection.

Tales of hacking, madness and obsession on the electronic frontier.

M&M, ZDNet, Kit Kat, Gizmodo, Pop Rocks, TechRadar, Circus peanuts, Gamasutra.

Eloonie Musk, Murky Cyberberg & Shakin' That Assteven Hawking: Space Is The Place.

Intergoofism, white collar computer crimes and the Lederhose deniable encryption program.

Adam and E.

Lost in music.

CHIC: Le Geek.

Texas Über Alles.

This Is A Recording.

Tigers don't fancy Esso at all.

RUN DSM-5: Walk This Way!

Breakfast in America Can Wait.

The Only Cure Is The Cure Itself.

Google Live And More Encore Plus.

A New Microsoft World Is At Hand.

Atomic Dogma 95: The Celebration.

Trump On Nukes, Trump On Nikes.

Jerry Halliday: Itsy Bitsy Petit Bikini.

And who carries the burden of shame?

Sun gonna shine on everything you do.

God Blast The United States of America!

Trump 2017: Mirror Mirror On The Wall...

Ay-in' the darkness must come out the light.

ExxonMobil: Fuelling journeys, powering lies.

Eros is a God to be honoured, not slaughtered.

The Madonnald's Menu: Sox, Fries and Videotape.

Now New At Madonald's: The Like A Virgin Burger.

All those in the memorial tombs of e will... come out!

LSDelicious: 60 Republican recipies based on insects.

Alex 'Jim' Jones: The Infowars Cult Conspiracy Years.

What kind of rhum should I use for my lawnmower/garden equipment?

Teddie's Love Cruz in the Paris Texas Hilton Hotel of Evangelical Needs.

www.shell.com | More About Shell. Who We Are. What We Do. Our Values.

Worldwide, you'll find rats near every MacDonald's restaurant, all jokin' aside.

Sarah Palin & The Sensational Cyberspace Shifters: 24 Hour Tea-Party People.

We need to embrace time lost as gain, as bliss, as freedom, as that's entertainment!

Sheila E.

Beast of Burden.

Walking in space.

Why Computers Die?

Metro, Boulot, MacDo.

Status Quo: FileDriver.

Bitch I'm Marissa (A. Mayer).

Ducks really don't dig Disney.

iPhone-6-2PAC: All i's On I.T.

(It'z) WAR: Deliver The Word.

Mortituri Te Salutant, Billi-Wifi!

I'm a Digibête and I'm proud of it.

Controlling life, controlling nature.

Capitalist numerology is meaningless.

Lady Gagagosian – Fame Eau de Toilet.

How Zuckerberg's world will be removed.

Apple: Rotten Fruit For Fresh Vegetables.

Bonjour. Esso est toujours proche de vous.

We Live In A Quantum Computer Universe.

Psychiatry, internet, buddhism, scientology.

In the Electronic Peepshow of Natural Desire.

Scritti Politti: The Microsoft 3rd Eye Word Girl.

Pope Francis: Strawberry Mojito Punch Dreams.

TIDAL eat your heart out, that is if you had any....

All those in the memorial tombs of e will... come out.

The Great Flashing Gordon's Gin Campbell Soup Swindle.

Prince Charles & The London City Beat Band: Cash Money.

Why Federico Fellini never wanted to make a film in the US.

Big, bigger, biggest, biggestest, biggissima, biggissimultissima.

Merely tryin' to survive in the Kim Kardashian Hotel of Mental Butt Implants.

Prince Charles Saatchi & The Brides of Windsor: We're Only Making Plans For Nigel.

Ich Glotz CCTV.

View all answers.

Lambchop: Nixon.

Next time die for free!

State of Independence.

Elimination, Illumination.

Saint Francis Ford Coppola.

Request an Uncle Sample kit.

An Halal Internet is on its way.

Ziggy Zizzette around the corner.

Air Force One Asshole Too Many.

What's ahead is a different colour.

Madonnald Trump: Like A Rapist.

Private jets are for public enemies.

Mice don't ever mention Micky Mouse.

Steve Jobs: L'homme qui portait malheur.

Paris (Hilton) Les Champs Elysilicônisées.

Jerry LSDee Lewis: Great Balls of FireWire.

Guten Abend. Esso ist immer in Ihren Nähe.

One moment in QuickTime and you were there.

Compliance with the laws of e, all together now!

MAC (Miller) ft. Kendrick Lamar: Fight The Feeling.

Prince Roger: If it was just a dream call me a dreamer 2.

Federico Fellini: Io Credo I Tutto / I Believe In Everything.

Google: Don't let them change ya, or even try to rearrange ya.

NRA Teddie & The Love Cruz Patrol Brigade: God's Not Dead.

Britpop, EXTRA, Milky Way, YHOO (NASDAG), Cotton Candy.

In the Paris Milton (Friedman) Hotel of Neoliberal Foundation.

It's all about size today, size and speed, size and speed and status.

CIA-B-C: The Bill & Roberta Gates Foundation Nation Part 1,2,3.

Hey, George H. & W. & DJ Jeb!: Ain't That Funkin' Kind Of Hard On You?!

Dennis The Menace & The Stone Age Coyote Hopper All-Stars: Oozi Rider.

My son was a gaming addict and shot 11 people at a nearby cinema, mostly kids.

S.C.U.M.M.M.M.: Society for Cutting Up Men, MacBooks, Microsoft, Mousepads.

Heidi Cruz: Wir wollen niemals auseinandergehen (We Never Want To Be Apart).

Blue Independence: 1½ oz. Bombay Gin, 1 oz. Blue Curacao, 2 oz. Mobil Jet Oil 254.

Janet Jacksonian Epilepsy Bitch Band: Control (And That's Where They Wanna Go!).

Edipe e.

Location of I.

Do Not Bend!

In the picture.

Call Carl Jung.

Art is for Brutes.

Cruzy Like Da US.

Die Like An Eagle.

Tant qu'il y aura des hommes.

Can Art History digest net.art?

On The Trump Trail of Unreason.

Black Mozart: Requiem in D Minor.

When the spaghetti hits the fan of e.

Fly Like An Igloo, Die Like An Eagle.

Big Goes The Bang and gone are the bugs.

America and the pornography of the heart.

Now I'm out in public and everyone can see.

A Guide To 7706 Emails In 2 Hours And 56 Minutes.

Breathing seals make the best pillows to have lovely dreams.

Seal: And we're never gonna survive if we don't get a little crazy.

Yes We Have No Banarama Rama Hare Hare Anti-Krisha Today!

McMick, McBlair, McDonna, McDonald, McBranson, McTrump.

Heino Cruz: Mit freundlichen Grüßen (With Friendly Greetings).

Get lucky.

Solid as a rock.

L'Enfant Sauvage.

Atomic Bomber Man.

What a waste of time.

What's Gates' Kingdom?

Don't you start bugging me.

Draw Close To Gates In Prayer.

Integration, not desintegration.

Rock, salt, water, sand, memory.

Legal uploads, illegal downloads.

Dr. Jekyll some & Mr. Hide others.

What is Bill's Purpose for the Earth?

Beyond morality lies the miracle of understanding.

Extinguishing the fire in the world, that's all there's to it.

This day in History: Anniversary of the Ice Cream Sundae.

Bill sends his angel and shuts the mouth of the lions of hack.

Eradication of Supa Dupa Riches is really the real challenge.

Names, trademarks, logos, designs, text, graphics and more of the same.

JP Gaultier sparkling table water and the meaning of your digital baptism.

Rusty.

I'll be right back.

Give it time, we all need time.

Double Donny: Crazy Horses.

The Scream (Flip To Play Loud).

Black Bison Radio Dream Time Out.

Swimming with dolphins in the salty deep.

Water and rust are a way to eat technology.

Kilobytes, megabytes, gigabytes, metabytes.

Below the bible-belt of world endings soon now.

Remember, no matter where you go online, there you are.

Internet, melancholia and the paleo psychoanalysis of dreams.

MacArthur Park, born again Christians and White Lord Creator Disorder.

Dysphoric and elevated mood, pre-lithic pipe smoking and the Brides of Funkenstein.

Open Source Mediocrity, Stone Age Schizophrenia and the Internet as institution of captivity.

Got it!

Happy...

The Dude.

Time slips away.

Homo factus est.

Domestic Nature.

Perpetual Reality.

Staring At The Sea.

You've got a friend.

The Cure: Lovesong.

Thinking the animal.

I Would Die For You.

Engineered to go to Sea.

I Wanna Be Where You Are.

The American Way of Drive.

Restore your (bodily) system.

Panda Bear What Do You See?

The Garden of Earthly Deletes.

Bernie: Love-letters in the sand.

Now on MoZillatron FireFox TV.

What You See Is What You Want.

The hand of the government man.

Swing it, shake it, move it, make it.

Roy Lichtenstein's Sun never rises.

Explaining Funk To The North Sea.

Out of the womb of Aquarius we crawl.

The online incarceration of wilderness.

A world already out of balance big time.

Mother Nature calls for peace as priority.

The Calcutta Botanic Garden, now online.

Craving for the news, good or bad, but really good.

Letting the days go by, let the water hold me down.

Letting the days go by, water flowing underground.

Vincent & Rolf Sunflowerbomb Eau de Toilet 50 ml.

McTopia, McTodd Rundgren and Congo Immersion.

The end of time will dissolute into the rivers below zero.

Going from fire into water requires lots from lots of people.

What Next?

Sorting stuff out.

Why even look at animals?

Seventeen Seconds: A measure of life.

The Nation's busiest death penalty state.

Deus Ex Machina (God From The Machine).

Drowning by the thousands, and it's just news.

Taha, Khaled, Faudel – Ya Rayah Live 1,2,3 soleils.

Koonsified, sanctified, commodified, commercialized.

IMB's Deep Blue poison dart frogs coming home to boast.

Hades sleep disturbance and Trump Mask Replica over again.

The Widow of Sorrow and her Tomato Trillion Dollar Beef Noodles.

Autostop, Miss Dooda, Gordon Cooper, Pin-Up Girl, Space Guardians.

Gorilla, Molly Peeters, Ice Cream 2, Happy Landing, Mocca Standard Station.

Brazilian salmon tarantula, Buffalo Zoo rainforest and the Deepwater Horizon Oil Spill.

All I have to say minus a few thoughts about the world I live in with you and with others.

Death denied.

God Only Knows.

Too late for tears.

Gone but not forgotten.

Yippee-ki-yay Motherf*cker!

When the Saint comes crashing in.

How to help! I need somebody to love.

Whitney Houston, we have a problem.

Turning away, and coming back again.

Concept of drugs in Pre-Hispanic Mexico.

Apps, add-ons, sidebars, toolbars, barflies.

Little Tony Berlusconi: The Dwarf Caimano.

Fire:Fox TV is already running with Old Nick...

Madonna ft. Damien Hirst: The Immaculate Heart.

Adam and The Giant Anteaters: Stand and Deliver!

Self-portrait as Space Bison, and a gorilla from Mars.

Sign up for the newsletter and get 10% off your next order.

Uncle RAM & Second Daft Punk Division: Random Access Miseries.

Microsoft Corporation, 1 Microsoft Way, Redmond, WA 98052-6399.

Bush Doc, I got a headache and you give me Pentobarbital... what is this?

About Andy.

Up, Up and Away.

For Heaven's Sake!

Alone Yet Together.

Arriving in Reverse.

The pursuit of oblivion.

Helping the plants breathe.

I am a deeply superficial person.

My best lines were never written.

Burger King Giant Size $1.59 each.

Bringing dead bodies to the digital city.

Concerning my own skull: Diamonds on the inside.

Sending in the Dotcommon Squirrel Monkey Murder Squad.

Rewriting Warhol: Ginger e Fred Blood Orange Krach 14 times in Yahoo.

Space Safari, Cruise Ship Vacation games and giant South-American river turtles.

For The Love Of Bob: Platinum, diamonds and Geldof's teeth extracted in magic ritual.

Stupid is as stupid does.

Starbucks and vampire bats.

I'm gonna start all over again!

It will come in time, you just be patient.

Nature on display in soap commercials online.

Seventeen Seconds To Mars: This Is Psychosis!

Buying realtime crackers to feed elephants online.

Love in the logic of war, and war in the logic of love.

Live8 Elvises, psychoactive eagle and origins of shamans.

Utopian orderings at the psychiatric facility nearest to you.

Carpe diem. Seize the day, boys. Make your lives extraordinary.

Paleo-Indian Peacock Soft shelled turtles bathing in the Memory Motel online.

We are the Giant Size Teenage Mutant Ninja River Turtle Dance Squad coming to town!

Seascape #1.

Life is sweet.

Macintoshiba VD.

Rich little poor girl.

Leave the Atom alone.

Sun sun sun, here we come.

Technology is a queer thing.

Deus Tyrannosaurus Rex Macchina.

The Green Coca-Cola Bottles River Killer.

EMojique sends the package to the American man.

Funkhansa Crashteam Reunion, but yes, a reunion.

The effect of Online Palaeontology on the teenage brain.

The knack of so arranging the world we don't have to experience it.

BIFF, Wrecking Ball, NRA Rhythm Nation, Jay ZZ Top Over The Pops.

25 Cats Named Uncle Sam and One Blue Pussy Cat Called Riot Control.

Digital wallpaper, American Sidekick turtles and Dinosaur gun violence statistics.

Technological progress has provided us with more than efficient means to go backwards.

Rewriting Warhol: Big Electric Cheerleader (silk screen ink on polymer paint on canvas).

HAIR.

Blue screen of death.

When they took my soul.

This Could Be (Come) Paradise.

You can set your Apple watch by it.

Navigating the Pacific was more complicated.

The sun's gonna shine on everything you do too.

The American Psychiatric (Up Your) Association.

Apple Inc. was founded on April Fools' Day, 1976.

Klaus Kinski is Wozniak in a film by Werner Herzog...

Daddy Ronald Lainglegs coming to Psycho Town to sort us out.

The slain Minotaur will break through the spatial wall of Science.

The terrible thing of the sun is it shines on everybody and everything.

The real problem is not whether machines think but whether men do.

Technology presumes there's just one right way to do things and there never is.

To make machines what they ought to be, the slaves, instead of the masters of men.

Man is a slow, sloppy and brilliant thinker; the machine is fast, accurate and stupid.

Education makes machines which act like men and produces men who act like machines.

Back to backups.

The Hotdog Menu.

Was this page useful?

Password Protecting Prophecies.

The Selecter: Celebrate The Bullet.

Uncle Clamshell-shocked the nation.

Don't get locked out of your life! (I did).

NRAmerica: How to create a bullet list?

How to erase my past and start up another one?

Peter Sellers bloopers and Pink Panther outtakes.

Ian Dury & The Blockheads: New boot up and panties.

There's a Highway into poverty, but barely a sidewalk out.

The Internet is the most powerful magnifier of slack ever invented.

Trying to embrace the darkness in which we swim, in which we swim.

Television to brainwash us all and Internet to eliminate any last resistance.

Dreamsz.

Only love.

Karma Police.

Kick it to the curb.

Come give me your sweetness.

The Nuclear MacBook Family.

Get that smile off your user interface!

Ancestral knowledge resists technology.

The Barbara Bushmen are a nasty bunch.

In Polynesia, when we fought face to face.

Stop Force Touching me you drooling ape!

Happy so happy the day I'll have you home.

Trackball, TransFlash, Transceiver, Transformer.

Come bring me your softness, comfort me through all this madness.

You can't take something off the Internet — it's like taking pee out of a pool.

Sgt. Pepper's Lonely Hearts Club Wideband Code Division Multiple Access.

The Internet is the world's largest library. It's just that all the books are on the floor.

Flash Drive, Paleo-Indian Tent Turtles, David Beckham's medium and long haircuts.

Touchsmart.

System halted.

PowerPC to the people.

Unhiding some, unblocking others.

When we're dancing close and slow.

News Feeds and other dog's dinners.

The Television Marquee Moonie Sect.

The dark has always been my way home to the light.

A journey of a thousand sites begins with a single click.

River Phoenix-Award BIOS Help and simulation games.

The Boss, Top Dog, Hugo Boss, She's The Boss, iBomber3.

The Net treats censorship as a defect and routes around it.

Peter Toshiba Salt-N-Pepa-N-Vinegar: Let's talk about sex.

Getting information off the Internet is like taking a drink from a fire hydrant.

Information on the Web is subject to the same rules and regulations as a conversation at a bar.

Saint Hilaire.

Trending Tropics.

Modify your account.

Do Not Touch The Holy Madman!

Kinks, lonely out there in the Pacific.

Living inside your online bank account.

Clinging on to the gold foot of my Father.

Where photographers think they are Vermeer.

Kanye West for IKEAssholes in the Garden of Edun.

Laurel & Hardy, Gilbert & George, Hewlett & Packard.

Social Oompha's Loompha's and random friends invites.

Are we smart enough to know how smart our animals are?

400 million people watching Ronaldo MacDonaldo Trampère Ubus.

TwitPic, Thyrax, Qwitter, Twitterific, Pinterest, terrified out of my wits.

Marketing anti-depressants, Facebook purity add-ons and fake celebrity death reports.

The Wire.

Talk Talk.

Barrabas Bush.

Asteroid Freddie Mercury.

Leaving my soul to Science.

Let me take you down 'cos...

Send Pere Ubu songs to your cell.

It takes high techno low iQ2 tango!

Joan Armatrading: Never Is Too Late.

Time heals only the wounds you show.

When the real bisons come crashing in.

Fast delivery, free returns, money back.

You are about to be redirected to: America.

Baking cakes on TV requires craftsmanship.

Lowlands Gorilla Paw and Updated Disorders.

Luxury gadgets for folks in need of the opposite.

Gaming compulsively for the need of a new Utopia.

We're making Paleo Psychotechnical Progress here.

Hail The Pharmaceutical Manufactures of America!

Research, treatment, diagnoses and capital punishment.

Navy Seals, DSM-5 Task Force and the invasion of Baghdad.

Punk, Pop Idol, Il Divo, The Aquatic Ape, The Durutti Column.

Zawinul's Weather Report predicts a firestorm, but a funky one in the end.

Start Dictation.

Across Atlantic Ice.

The Animal Within.

Before we ruled the earth.

Who do you think you are?

Bison eat burgers nowadays.

Why do bison roll in the dirt?

Chameleons no cross no zebras.

www: The (2nd) Coming of Man.

Dead men talk to each other online.

Welcome to the Appalachians Store.

Byte, risk, uncertainty and Paleo profit.

Being bony in the North American Spring.

In search of the first programming language.

The European Origins of American Thought.

There are actually 'people' behind the DSM-5.

Microsoft or the Anatomy of Industrial Order.

In search of the lost world of Hannah Montana.

The Cultural Life of the American Online Colonies.

McZuckerberg: The Ape That Took Over The World.

Password alternatives, Ice age crossings and pure wild bison.

Jeb Bush on the subject of commie, albino activists in the Caribbean.

Apple Merch, Feel Classic Forgotten Fools and basic facts about bison.

Order DSM-5, Björn Borg's Classic Loungewear and DSM-5 Collection here and now!

The David Deaf Metal Deodorant Dance Squad ft. Queen Victoria Beckham: Wannabe.

Björn Borg's Long Jee-Haa Johns and Haute Caveman Couture for GOP Presidential hopefuls.

The Present Age.

Being and Having.

Freedom of species!

The Immoral Molecule.

Into the forest of taboos.

The Restless Atmosphere.

On the Notion of Free Wifill.

Information and gravitation.

Live on Meister Eckhart Tolle TV.

Nature, Internet and human values.

Guns, burgers, dollars and disorders.

Shantih-virushing to the Altar of Love.

Dropped out, not running, dead in fact.

20.000 Wattson: Johnny Played Guitar.

Cell and Psyche: The Biology of Purpose.

There's no dignity or respect on the www.

The amputated alphabet of tech-language.

Dancing with wolves, waltzing with bisons.

On the internet, nobody knows if you're a dog.

The Rise of the new Paleo Psycho Puritanism.

A Certain American-Samoan Male Female Fat Ratio.

When you start to spend more time gaming than living.

We're JAMA, we're JAMA, we hope you like JAMA too.

From Myth to Logic, from Logic to RAM, from RAM 2 JAM.

New in store: The DSM-5 Shoe Collection (Support us on FB).

Rodham City.

Accept terms.

e! is everywhere.

Writing in images.

This Was America.

Water water everywhere.

The Innernet Revolution.

Errand into the wilderness.

The virtual invasion of Man.

Being way out of line, online.

Wearing the many masks of being alone.

The ocean is the answer to all pornography.

Introduction to a Metaphysic of Desillusion.

Self-portrait of a puritan merchant in Cleveland Ohio.

The world wide scope of demythologising our humanity.

Like a Calvin Klein Jeans Infinite Indigo Candle in the wind.

Internet Gaming Disorder and the Online Presence of Eternity.

If bits could fly.

My hips don't lie.

Between the ears.

My bones don't lie.

The name is Jupiter...

The related Crisis in Art.

Bones tell stories you know.

Full of spite, byte and Sprite.

More questions than answers.

Bleaching bones, even my own.

Different routes to similar ends.

Motors, machines and messages.

Microsoft and Micropaleontology

Information and the Origin of Life.

The Internet is the Picadon of our time.

The White House Death Room Interior.

Fish know more than we do only we don't know it.

The Undersea Innernet is inaccessible for humans.

Bill Gates' search for common ground between God and technological evolution.

Rain of Iron, Ice and RAM, the very real threat of online comet and asteroid bombardment.

F* This!

The Sea of iCe.

Before The Flood.

Spoiled on canvas.

Pietá, P-Funk, Picadon.

Intel Swimwear Partner.

Your system status is serious.

I left my cellphone in Chicago.

Snapshots of spoken language.

Create Your FREE What Now?!

Welcome to the Virtual Vespiary.

USA: Where more money counts.

Dutch Internet Mountain and Sea.

How to make stone iTools from flint?

The End of Sorrow is (not) yet in sight.

Computer language and speech defects.

Pop Art, Trashthetics, Stone Age America.

The Amish Stewart Peoples: Knock On Wood.

The North American Soil Color Card for iPhone6.

In Bangkok they say Hillary Clinton is a she-male.

American Moon, 50 Shades of Dre, size not specified.

Stone arrowheads, bone arrow points and force quit applications.

Adolf Wölfli's Campbell's Tabasco Soup, now in Stone Age America.

Detected threats, left over Smart uninstaller and The Flint Knapper.

Sgt. Slim Cessna Auto Toto Club Band: With a little help of my friends.

The prehistoric exploration of the WordWildWeb and its place in the cosmos.

These massive seagulls picked my eyes out halfway on the Internet Mountain.

Native American artefacts, Samsung Galaxy S6, diamond-encrusted buffalo skulls.

Insect movement, Sepik River Clay, Papua New Genesis and Windows 10 upgrades.

Beaks of byte picking at my cojones of resistance, at the foot of the Internet Mountain.

Empowering us all.

Keep your head up.

How to make a bow?

Keep your heart strong.

Finding Flint Eastwood.

Why do I need to sign in?

Your potential. Our passion.

Apple, awards and accolades.

Fame n' Shame, Fame n' Shame.

Like Farrah Fawcett without a face.

Create as many questions as you like.

The Deadlock Holiday Disk-Drive Inn.

The Native Indian Flint Festival of Tools.

What is the point of talking crap like that?

Check out the most amazing celebrity fun acts.

Sit back and relax; you have free protection for life.

Everything in New York ain't always what it seems.

Mac, Pepsi, Redbone, James Brown, The Residents.

Apple Certified pear-to-pear applications 11 times in orange.

Rewriting Warhol: Camarillo Brillo Soap pads for Protestants.

Victory 1: Baby Bubba To The Boogie Da Bang Bang The Woogie.

Victory 2: I Gotta Boogie To The Woogie, Say Up Jump Da Boogie.

What you watch on your PC tells you what your life's supposed to be.

McMacTV.

Go Where You Flow.

Eyes like wild flowers.

Message from a drum.

Prozac is just your happiness.

In The Memory Cleaner Hotel.

Donny Trump Unplugged 2016.

Share Your #CalvinKleinMinute.

Simplifies memory control over your life.

Nice Dollar Green Curtains you got there!

There is literally nothing out there for you.

Windows OX 10 and mixed blood ancestry.

Biting Jeff Bezos in the Land of Zillatronopia.

Warhol's From A-Bomb to ZZ Top (and back).

The All The President's Men Size Movie Guide.

Solving the mysteries of the electronic evolution.

Candido Lolly Vasquez-Vegas for President 2016!

Decide yourselves where the bytes are taking you!

Bows and arrows and spearheads and files recovery.

I'm the Boneheaded Detective of the Paleo-US-World.

Marlon Brando redeems the United States on his own.

The Tinker-faced Queen-Bee Gossipmonger of Alabama City.

Sgt. Magic Slim Cessna Auto Da Funk Club Band: Black tornadoes.

Prehistoric Rhythm, Jimi Hendrix, Monica Lewinsky, George Clinton.

Dart points, knife blades, tomahawks and free antivirus scan in progress.

Last read.

Need help?

Driver's seat.

All Categories.

Cosmic Camera.

Mark Zipperberg.

Diggin' in the dust.

Samsing a songsung!

Monkey see, monkey double.

No more time, no more space.

Everything, everyday, all the time.

Videophone is rather uncinematic.

A download is shorter than a drink.

Sly & The Family Flintstone: Fresh.

Life is not always what you make it.

Digital stars make no Celestial Being.

Only cowboys watch Indians on the Net.

Desktops, notebooks and elephant birds.

A leopard doesn't change its spots online.

Multi-coloured feathers fly beyond death.

Bisons prefer a distant past, like we all do, no?

Windows everywhere, but not a house for rent.

Lord Shiva The Destroyer will save us, all 'n all.

Creation was like Program Creation, they think.

You want to get personal but you don't know how.

Online, wide open, confused, lonely and paranoid.

Because a PC makes noise even when switched off.

Too many people know too much about each other.

Get back in the game (I didn't know I was out of it!).

Celestial beings also float deep down the well of hell.

The ALLSDeBrazzas Monkey Circus of Soul Recovery.

Walkers, gliders, crawlers, swimmers, climbers, printers.

Thin Lizzy Taylor Swift ft. Kendrick Lamar: Paradise Lost.

The Internet is the mirror of mediocrity in times of misery.

Madness is not realising the limits of your mind, the limits of existence.

Rise.

View all.

Rise Again.

Are you now?

View nothing.

Licence to Bill.

The Power To Be Your Best.

I have a long purchase history.

Played by robots, scored by nature.

Dazzling growth, explosive expansion.

Billions and billions and billions of them.

15 Smart Junk Alternatives to Healthy Food.

Technology is the weakest link in technology.

Where privacy rights online die with the dead.

The dreaming experience you love, now for Mac.

Crossing the Interstyx you will find no tomorrow.

You're either crazy like them or you're crazy like us.

A couple hooked on a game while their child starved to death.

Pixar Picasso.

Exit Planet DOS.

Oysters and mobiles.

On a dark desert Highway...

You are better off not knowing.

The oceans keep rising anyway.

Like Bowlbeggar Bill-The-Bustonly.

When the horizon ascends into the sky.

Humanity is a simultaneous happening.

LSD, CEOs, fossils, origins and innovations.

America – The Final Countdown (with lyrics).

An ocean is an expert system developed by Teknowledge.

Information devices for universal, tyrannical, womb-to-womb surveillance.

Utilising Smartphones to Enhance Psychotherapy and Extend the Reach of Psychology.

How To?

Scroll to top.

My life as a disc

Microsoft People.

You can't escape it.

Get straight through.

A phone is a terrible thing.

A beauty case for the mind.

Digicash, Lascaux, hotlines.

Evil Empire & Space Odyssea.

Lord, I'm coming home to you!

FastForward thinking required.

Find a grave (browse by location).

Monks tweeting instead of praying.

Do Androids Chase Electric Sheep?

The Net rests on the water's surface.

Digital nature is not good for anyone.

Order your Chinchilla Sandwich here.

The Internet of Me, the Internet of You.

In terms of compliance with the enemy.

Good ice cream you get in Italy, sur place.

American Bison and Online Surveillance.

Cause marketing and the clearance of guilt.

If the television generation was a grim bunch...

Weather, games, screen, flickr, mobile, finance, more.

I have read and agreed to these terms and conditions.

Back to Life.

Ready or not.

Prêt-a-Porter.

Bitter Lennon.

MacStore Cowboy.

Here comes success.

This is not language.

A PC is a mouse trap.

Every PC has a grave.

Poverty creates sadness.

Get with the space program!

Home space for the homeless!

What are data-protection laws?

We inhabit the world now, finally!

Time for a bit of folder iconoclasm.

Lord of the Birds, Lady of the Bites.

Rock paintings and reverse markets.

What a wonderful world this could be.

My digital funeral was a real deception.

Morality is no longer in our own hands.

The Apple Boutique was run by The Fool.

Fake hallucinations for floppy individuals.

You may ask yourself... how did I get here?

Light a candle for the dead on the following website.

Thinking your thoughts and sending them off by pressing your temples.

In Edgefunds.

Earth Perfect?

WORLD TOTAL.

The law of large numbers.

The eWheel of Misfortune.

Can't read this simcard at all!

I loved queuing for the cinema.

Ground Control to Uncle Jam.

We now think the computer is flat.

Chinatown is where Microsoft eats.

Apple's driving me bananas, obviously.

Driverless cars make great ghost-drivers.

You can fool some people some of the time –

But you can't fool everybody all the time America.

Bison latrifrons and natural language voice-commands.

Slow drip, Wifi inside, pool of tears, Xanadu, Patty Hearst.

Me, MyGlass, myself, & I No (Yes!) New Holland Lady Corry DADA.

Uncle Jeb's White Rice Jazz Bushband & Google X-Ray Ban All Stars: YEZZ!

Kellog's Psycho Pop's Soap-Oprah and Deep SixPak Chopra, together on a couch.

SPAMK!

Only love.

Sudan online.

The Age of Abuse.

Behind your back.

Beyond perfecting.

iPhone-6-packaging.

Sell me something good.

Stormy Travolta: Oh Sandy.

The statistics are staggering.

Welcome to The Cruel World.

We're all being cheated big byte.

Internet Penetration in Africa in 2018.

Internet growth and mental regression.

You ought to be buying right at this moment.

Virtual missiles to defend a warped Humanity.

Breaking news, local weather, original content.

Big MacBook Pro-Life: A Republican preference.

White DJ's, black markets, yellow pills, green deaths.

The Tubes at the Billy Graham Video Archive 1975-1979.

The Paul McCarthy Habsburger King Santa Claus Kinskin I'm in!

MacBooks, mammoths, mastodons, camels, horses and ground sloths.

Barry White & The Unlimited Story Capacity Orchestra: I'm Qualified...

The WorldWideWeb flashes the Hell of Existence, or the Existence of Hell.

Club Mad.

Right now!

Back to '78.

The Detector.

Quality Quick.

Continue Reading.

Simplify your journey.

Logos, insults, slogans.

Popular in your network.

The End of Handwriting.

Go VIP for free downloads.

Bison antiquus, Google Glass.

All similar to the issue of water.

The Cyclones of Dr. Funkenstein.

Lost, lonely and littered with spam.

The Genocide of Culture continued.

Quicktime is an insult to the Universe.

People with no money are better dancers.

All the many many ways Big Brother is watching you.

Ensuring freedom, security and grow in our digital world.

More than 3 billions minds aligned at the same moment in time.

Habsburgers & McNuggets: The Last Vienna Merchandays of Mankind.

Giant Ice Age Bison and MacBook Air 13 Inch (I Need 13 Inches or more).

The diarrhea of Virtuality leaking into my severely damaged brain train 24/7 all year round.

Turn it off.

Skies Of Fire.

Gamin on ya!

Access denied.

StyleClickStart.

Adolescent Sex.

Turn if off, I said.

Owls stay out of I.T.

Wasted and Wanted.

The Calling Sickness.

Warm smell of colitas.

Services and standards.

Money. Power. Respect.

Inner Circle: Mary Mary.

Through The Google Glass.

Killing, browsing, shopping.

Nothing to text home about.

Preaching to the megabytes.

The way of the white iClouds.

Blurred lines: physical|digital.

The Pious Bird of Good Omen.

Wipe that smiley of my screen!

McManual of Mental Disorders.

'Apres lui le déluge.' Paris Match.

Lies, spies and spiders on the wall.

A baboon wearing the moon is real.

Ordinary men, ordinary computers.

We were once 1.000 people on this earth.

John Kerry: Beanz Meanz America 2016!

PC, profit, Pepsi, people, psychiatry, poodles.

Diapers.com (We ship now to +65 countries!).

Please McWrap The White House Mr. Christo!

Roll-out, learn more, see what's possible, flash...

Visit Your Country Site (or rather the countryside).

The Arab spring turned out to be the winter of Islam.

Fibre Optica de Telmex, Christine Le Duc, Product (RED), Adidas.

A Royal Filet-O-Fish McZuckerBurger to Make America Greed Again!

My Personal Paleo Psychosomatic Funk Circus Therapy against net-addiction.

The 2016 refugee crisis and Christiano Ronaldo's best hairstyles for that same year.

X-Factor.

Cut The Crap.

So many roads.

Alive in America.

Yeah! Yeah! Yeah!

Always On The Run.

Many cables to cross.

Macaques and MacBooks.

Good morning Mr. Orwell!

I heard the news today oh boy.

What happened, Miss Simone?

Nobody asks Ringo anything, ever!

I'm gonna stand by my laptop now.

The Google Chromosome Disasters.

I'm NOT free NOT to do want I want!

Motown: The Sound of Young America.

For we all came forth from earth and water.

World Bank affairs and more hippie modernism.

The Great Slaughter of the American Bison Herds.

Next – Shopping in Nigeria: An amazon.com for Africa?

Uncle Ben Carson's Country Inn Rice (#BeginWithBen).

My Mama Said.

Keep your mind set.

www: Sicko Curiosity.

The edge of Darkness.

We are IN a Cyberwar.

Like a Will Smith movie.

Hot of the press no more.

Gerber son wifi fait mal à personne.

Johnny Lydon: Anger is my energy!

A Solar Flare will end the Internet big time.

Meet Mr. Mitnick, the world's most famous hacker.

The Very Best of Trump – 50 Unforgettable Tracks.

'I love the Mexican people, they're rapists, like myself.'

Uncle Bernie's Socialist Black Rice To The Presidency.

Pokémon Go Jungle! Go Jungle! Go Join Your Gang Yeah!

Trampled Underfoot: The power and excess of Led Zeppelin.

If the Internet goes down, people will not remember how life was before it.

Silence...

Driven to discs.

Trump on torture.

Not a second time.

Shoot me a psy-mail!

Fame Who's to Blame?

Connective depression.

Bursting the banks of e.

Young capital, old game.

iDrinks and PC-dinners.

e in the Sahara, with you.

Coffins and blockbusters.

Water versus Electronics.

Turning my digital stomach.

I'm pushing my wheel of love.

Your partner in climax solutions.

The rich eradicating poverty, great.

Single shot, double pounder, triple X.

Meet the real Eric Weiss, Mr. Mitnick!

Chi-mails, con-shells and burrito wraps.

Cage Against The Machine: eVil eMpire.

The Internet does not make a good story.

Patterns in chaos that shouldn't be there?

On The Road.

Happy together.

Risen from the Net.

Thinking frustration.

Toshiba Salt & Vinegar.

Insane in the midbrain.

Recession is always hot.

Dial (Da) Dalai Lama Now.

Hacking the neighbor's dog.

How many tears in a microchip?

Delete History, remember nothing.

Eye-contact is essential to teaching.

Reprogram your television, or die trying.

It's all visual noise, and not just a bit of it.

Earth, Wind, Fire, Ether, Schweppes, 7UP.

The food chain has become completely dependent on I.T.

We have all data on terrorist fish in the Pacific at this moment in time.

Risen already.

Lost Highway.

OS, the people.

Prior to encryption.

L'instant Microsoft.

Show your Windows.

(Shut up) I'm loading!

The sick say go slower.

Formatting my religion.

A Room with an iTVIEW.

Language devoid of feeling.

Big wheels keep on turning.

The Highway forever draws away...

On Free Will and (Free) Downloads.

Wimbledon in Space: Darth Federer.

The Facebook Priscilla Chan Ltd. Clan.

Dumping digital into the souls of humans.

Ram shoulder-bone divination and digital delay.

Jeb Bush: 'My mom is the strongest woman I know.'

Nico Kidman & The Volvo Underground: Down Under.

Microsoft's backdoor-entry to Outlook, Hotmail, Skype.

Web, images, video, news, local, answers, shopping, more.

Let's go out and buy some Native American Ceremonial Spears!

The latest.

The future?

Proxy magic.

Brilliant trees.

Fesses 2 fesses.

I want a baboon!

The Digital Divide.

Finding anomalies.

Innovation at work.

Cyberattacking Mars.

Whiling away spare time.

The Anonymity Network.

Baby you can drive my car.

Let's Talk About Your Hair.

Talking about a resolution...

Pop is over when you want it.

I can't feel anything anymore.

Does your conscious bother you?

America Eats Its Young Americans

Disconnected life, undisturbed soul.

Netflixing you out of house and home.

Reality TV Stars and castration anxiety.

Programming Spectacled Langur Language.

I came to Mexico to make contact with the Red Earth.

Seemingly feeding the young, the poor and the miserable.

Place struck by lightning consecrated to Larry Mullen Jr.

Serpents burnt alive, Pretzel Logic and luxury lifestyle gadgets.

Rock 'n Roll Over Beethoven Mr. Wolfgang Amazon.COMozart!

Corporate America or The Patisserie of Civil Cowboy Corruption.

In our bone-circus, left alone with each other, and ourselves, you and me.

Netflixing, match fixing and flat-out P-Funking you around the block of Reason.

This is a fierce bad robot, look at his savage whiskers, and his claws, and his turned-up tail.

Join this conversation!

Can't see this message?

This Is What You Want.

Installing... please be patient...

I see this life like a swinging vine.

Uncle Jeb's Rice-Pops is killer food!

Arabic Speaking Internet Infiltration...

Welcome to My World (John Travolta).

Charlie & The Foxconn Suicide Factory.

Earth, Wind, Fire, Water, Ether & Facebook.

The Plains Indians Peoples' return to the table.

Mario Rubio: 'We put in 110% and still get screwed!'

The Paranoid Self, Behind The Screens, Like A Prayer.

iPad Air U2, iPad Mini U3, iPut The Funghi On The Trigger.

Franz Ferdinand I & The McHabsburger Orchestra: TASTE IS KING!

Weather, Copyrights, Telecom Reports, Papa Don't Preach, Tomatoes on Mars.

Fined Again!

Bits in space.

Freedom to create.

Elsewhere is otherwise.

iCentre of the Universe.

I do think the world is sold.

(Don't) let your dreams die.

The Internet is out of control.

Mind reading through the www.

Takes 2 to do the Turings Tango.

Take that money (watch it burn).

Americans are one-way thinkers.

Everything is coming to a grinding halt.

Everything that kills me makes me feel alive.

Michael Jackson Pollock: Man In The Mirror.

31 billion devices connected to the internet in 2020.

Republican discussion of bison protection is non-existent.

Another life.

Cloning kills.

Lost To Tech.

Different world.

Artificial Stupidity.

This moment in time.

AC/DC Pinball Rocks HD.

Actual size is hard to guess.

Maradona was a line driver.

Eat This, Not That, But This!

A plea for an offline Humanity.

Grand Funk Information Railroad.

The Karaoke Revolution Party Program.

On the Net you never feel really welcome.

We help protect over 2.5 billion hamburgers.

Loss of land, food source and spiritual effects.

The price of concert tickets has become an issue.
Cow wallpaper, quasi-intelligence and Diet Coke.
Bison priscus, MacBook Pro, Basquiat, Vogue Magazine.
Ronald Reagan: Standing In The Light (Full Album 1984).
iTunes: Our Top 10 Presidential Candidates For September.
Microsoft Mon Amour and other modern bison resurgence efforts.
€=mc².
Scare Me.
Restraint.
Shame on us.
Point and shoot.
No easy way out.
In full remission.
Le Louvre online.
(WHAT) About Us.
Lonely over the top.
Still waters run deep.
Eternal fame, everyday.
Security, security, security.
Just another nervous wreck.
Did Jobs really care about you?
Combat Mission: Shock Forces.
Just missed my Kodak moment.
How Gates Answers Our Prayers.
The Google X-Rated iMovie Guide.
Living In A Way That Pleases Gates.
A splendid time is guaranteed for all.
Is Schmidt uncaring and hardhearted?
Comcast, Outkast, Cumcost, California.
Disney dinnerware for dippy dilettantes.
Don't push us 'cos we're close to the edge.
U2 & Apple: A m@tch m@de in H€AV€N.
Dreams are (not) meant to remain dreams.
The Western BBQ Habswhopper Monarchy Mausoleum.
Programming Language and other means of communication.
The Habsburger King Hot Brownie-Shirts (NEW IN STORE).
Status God.
Let me ride.
Take a walk.

Think Small.

Quality time...

I am modified.

Built for speed.

Counting Stars.

Not Now I said!

Are we all dead?

Only everything.

Too sad to Skype.

You. Only smarter.

Some dance to forget.

The Walrus has left us.

Beyond Good and Euro.

Recommended For You.

Having this, we want that.

Solutions for a small planet.

Create your Apple Identity?

Printing my testament in 3D.

Change is the erosion of memory.

Singing songs about the southland.

Sorry, I'm not online, do you mind?

Armani Mania and offline depression.

Race Against The Messiah: Refill Empire.

The Great Internet Traffic Report Swindle.

Between the Devil and the IBM Deep Blue.

Use of the darknet, under cover of the night.

Dead is the Hudson, long live the Sepik River!

Sacrifice to Tim Cook for the fruits of the land.

Stinging With The Blue Ants Of Volcanic Funk.

There is no such person as the Nijinsky of Virtuality.

Pre-orders, damage cases and post-natal depressions.

The Confetti of Commerce are the Cumshots of Consumption.

Da buzz, da money, da junk, da bubble, da bullshit, da depression.

The wind in my heart

The wind in my heart, the dust in my head...

The dust in my head, the wind in my heart, the wind in my heart...

Try Now!

Open Happiness.

Access restricted.

Get out of my life.

The Berlin Screen.

Can't sleep anymore.

Cool wind in my hair.

I'm the great Descender.

Don't go with the data flow!

Tell me that I'm drumming.

Crazy computer scientists going nutz.

The Internet dreaming itself: Bollocks part 3.

The warlike, underground uprising of all bones.

Frrrrrrrrranzzzzzzzzz Beckenbauer: Ein Leben Als Fussballer.

The Digital Haves and the Have-nots and the Have-nothing-at-alls.

Fossiles, dinosaur leg-bones and Internet World Penetration Rates.

Transmigration of digital souls into virtual turtles and online bears.

Tim Cook & Silicon VD All-Stars: I'm coming out, I want the world to know.

Navy Fix: 1½ oz. Sauza Blue Silver Tequila, Coca Cola Life, silicone fluids, boric acid.

Decline.

Electro Ladyland.

The Hotdog Menu.

Ah yes, reading books....

Social nature has changed.

Tags, videos, images, categories.

Password Protecting Prophecies.

Live in your world. Play in theirs.

Uncle Clamshell-shocked the nation.

Van Halen: Running with the iPhone.

The Plasmatic Wendy Williams Show.

Tony! Get On Da Mike! (Blair Witch Dub).

EMojique buys equipment in the market place.

What the country needs are a few labor-making inventions.

Television to brainwash us all and Internet to eliminate any last resistance.

FLOW-MATIC BeanShell & EusLisp Robot Programming Language spoken.

Technological progress has provided us with more than efficient means to go backwards.

Bug Mac.

Life Is A Dance.

All is Interstellar.

You Are My Kind.

Advertise with us.

iPizza Dunce Nights.

How big is your world?

A friend, like Ben Harper.

Infiltration = penetration.

The Wounds of the World.

15-day trial period expired.

Can you do the camel walk?

Kesiah Jones: My kinda girl.

Intra Circle: Magic Machine.

Zapp and Roger Live in Aruba.

The Seven Chips of Happiness.

Herds of robots comin' our way.

A psychopath in cheap's clothing.

My screen just attacked me, Madame.

Grace and Kesiah Jones: Nightclubbing.

The hand goes only where the mouse goes.

Prisons have window systems installed too.

I'm gonna go to a private beach party with you.

Santana ft. Chad Kroeger: Why Don't You and I?

Gilbert & George ft. Aloe Blacc: (The) Blacc Man.

I'm sitting here watching the wheels go round and round...

Andy Warhol's polaroids of celebrities were the first selfies.

Coming Home: Counting Stars, Stripes, Coffins (The Bush Wars).

Twin Dutch Stellararities: Douwe Bobby Cash & Jett Rebel Rebel.

Get Hopi.

Youcision.

Often bought.

A girl so fine...

Rhythm is love.

Man in the Maze.

Labyrinth of Love.

Call I.T. What I.T. Is.

Keep it simple stupid.

Buy, buy, buy, buy, buy.

Whats-Your-Sign.com.

Yellow lives matter too.

Con Brio: Kiss The Sun.

Kesiah Jones: Where's Life?

You say you buy and I say hello!

Into the Sweatlodge of Unreason.

Coming of Age in my Adidas Samoa.

Wake me up before Van Gogh Gogh!

Mother's Finest: Another Mother FranknFurther.

Vlady Putin & The Bearskin All-Stars: Paristroikax.

Spastic Teddie Cruz' Machine-Gun Bacon, now $2.99!

Britney Spears Curious Eau de Parfum for witches the world over.

Adolf Wölfli & G-RAW ART BRUT All Stars: You're Under Arrest!

Nespresso Clooney and the Clowns of Fonkenstein: Coffee-Funk is tomorrow.

Walk this way.

I need a dollar.

In the Googleheim.

Defy Your Limitations.

L'Internet et Son Double.

Computers create solitude.

Your screen is your mirror.

Can you feel my heart beat?

Here is where the story ends.

The Cro-Magnon Gay Parade.

Today everybody has an opinion.

Crushed by the Wheels of Industry.

Dot consumption for mental zombies.

It takes the world to tango all together.

Hip-bones, übercodes and bison livers.

Finally we can all be geniuses together!

Sympathetic magic and digital security.

Facebook murders and twitter suicides.

George WC. Strawberry oilFields Forever.

Donna Summer, internet lobotomy and Werther suicides.

And other conditions that may be a focus of clinical attention.

Sirens, hackers, prophets, psychiatrists, cheerleaders, chief executives.

Today everybody has an opinion about anything anytime anyplace anyhow.

iApples.

Tweet Tweet.

The Last of Us.

True emojitions.

Where are you?!

Share Happiness.

Take a quick tour.

We have forgotten.

Trending yesterday.

Speed your love to me.

The Serpent and the Rainbow.

Remember the fast boot times?

The day they elect a virtual Pope.

Windows PowerShell Oil Nigeria.

Insomnia, insomnia, everywhere...

New York Telephone conversation.

Where the poor can think they're rich.

Beheading in iPhone 6 high resolution.

Major Tim Cookle: The Naked Launch.

The way app is the same as the way down.

Emperor Tamarin Marky Mark iZucker hamBurger II.

Funny Moments Donald Trump, ultimate compilation.

Today BABEL is a text generation subsystem by Margie.

End bullying in your school with online courses on peace education.

Saturday Night Live Monkey Families, looking at each other, online.

OK.

Contacts.

Rock solid.

More news.

Natureality.

I'm so alone.

What A Waste!

How does it feel?

Life is portable now.

Generals and majors.

Enhance your writing.

Streaming your afterlife.

Easy money, raging fools.

It's all in the mind you know.

My psychiatrist is a metalhead.

The Internet is 3.5 billion masks.

Smartphones facilitate terrorism.

You take the High-Res, I take the Low-Res.

King Cola Bio Yoghurt & Queen Pepsi Maxima.

Collaborative programming some call betrayal.

Why balloon help if you can ring an ambulance?

The ideal chance for your kids to grow into monsters they not yet are.

Uncle Ben Carson's White Rice GOP Jazz Orchestra: Eurosurgery (Club Mix).

Fred Flintstone & Paleo-All-Starliament Trumpadelic: One Nation Under A Hoof.

Bono Christ is also the only one whom Gates used when He created all other things.

Like and Loose.

I'm fixing a bug.

Earthworm Jim.

Return to Sender.

Going for Chrome.

Murdoch Most Foul.

Beyond the invisible.

I am a PC-Evangelist!

Video killed the radio star.

Thinking outside the Xbox.

Love. Fast. Easy. Anywhere.

Risk and prognostic feathers.

Shakin' with the Money Man.

Towards a world without feeling.

⅓ of China simultaneously online.

Welcome To The Yellow Stone Age!

Gates wants you to know who He is.

Hollywood is traditionally left-wing...

When Bono Christ told his fans to pray.

BioShock, Golden years, Dabble Dabble.

If the www would empty out its bellows...

Free as a bison some hundred fifty years ago.

Surviving on bison livers in the world of the Deepnet.

Not only the Times have changed, but Time itself as well.

When lizards talk to hyenas, Donald Trump is the translator.

Eagle totem clans, bison secret societies and Elevation board meetings.

Computer talk: a dangerous reduction of language, and destruction of soul.

I'm a mandrill copulating with the night-nurse in an ambulance down lover's lane.

Owl-faced Monkey traversing the internet with nocturnal autism spectrum disorder.

RIGGED!

About Computer Hope.

The Nuclear MacBook Family.

Polynesian Instant Messaging.

Money ain't got a thing on me!

I had a life once... now I have a computer.

Jebb! Time and tide will wait for no man.

Trackball, TransFlash, Transceiver, Transformer.

The Net treats censorship as a defect and routes around it.

Eros Ramazotti & Tony Thanatossi: Si Mi Falta Tu Mirada.

Apple Computer Inc., 1 Infinity Loop, Cupertino, CA 95014.

Talking about the future of the internet is highly speculative megalomania.

Back.

WIRED.

MEXICO!

Jailbreak 2.

All Authors.

Show more.

Bon appétit!

Say it isn't so.

AmbientTalk.

Recommended.

Reinventing Eden.

Please don't touch.

Machines don't love.

The Exploded Selfie.

Waltzing with robots.

Joy is something else.

Clean Up By Droning.

Speaking of polaroids.

Forgot your password?

Learn more, know less.

My 10.000 pen-friends.

The Mobile Revolution.

Steppin' in the slide zone.

Oops! Upside Your Head...

Sinnovation That Sexcites.

Codebreakers and codemakers.

Who's really nuts in this world?

Howler-Monkey Status Off-line.

What's The Name Of The Game?

Manic-recession searching my soul.

Looking at numbers instead of ideas.

Advertisement is set dressing in Hell.

Licking envelops was good, wasn't it?

The Digital Dark Age has commenced.

The Nile's too deep for your pop agenda.

One Big Cheese Habsburger Royal bitte!

NO to the lurking terror of soul destruction!

www is the worst enemy of critical thinking.

The world over the cliff of a nervous download.

Bruno Mars is the new James Brown, all joking aside :-).

It's alright.

Don't panic.

Bush-De-La!

Hard To Stop.

Back to the night.

We stand together.

The The: Mind Bomb.

Chocolate and Cheese.

Red Sails In The Sunset.

Stand up and be counted.

Leaving the world behind.

RHCP: Hump The Trump!

Exploding my drone-shield.

The new business diaspora...

Kraftwerk: Computer World.

Trump The World, Armorica.

Nothing's Shocking Anymore.

Music for the jilted generation.

Life is a song – love is the music.

Codify it in its Bill of Guarantees.

Right back where we started from.

The PC Police is coming to getcha!

Fewer genocides, more harassment?

Counting in the global bullshit factor.

Dance little sisters, dance little brothers!

We're all in the dark searching for the light.

We are social beings whether we like it or not.

The White Race? Leave Africa and hang a left.

The West Coast Pop Art Experimental Band Part 3.

Life is like music, it must be composed by ear, feeling and instinct, not by rule.

We need to sit together around a campfire every once in a while, noblesse oblige.

Blocked access to file-sharing sites and more allsdeceit-Trumpadelic non-sense.

Feel Up.

Do The Dog.

Still Believe.

Flash & Blood.

Come to my aid.

The Lobster Boy.

Brumes et pluies.

Subscribe to love.

Smileys are a zoo.

Rihanna is a rebel.

It's only rock'n roll.

Try something new.

Pretty Paracetamol.

Saturday Night Evil.

I fi, you fi, we all fi for wifi.

Soft mon amour, très soft.

Only the dream is left alive.

Working For The Rat Race.

LSDexy's: Come On Eileen!

I'm in my pink period peoples.

Ziggi Politti: The Sweetest Girl.

The internet equals non-feeling.

George Benson: Weekend in L.A.

Searching For The Space Monkey.

Robert Palmer: Looking For Clues.

Cat Stevens: I.T. For The Tillerman.

Smileys, animals and human nature.

Rock lobsters, set them free, ah yes…

Lost in the Barrio I walk like an Injun.

Bootsy's Ultra Wave: Play With Bootsy.

Rewriting Warhol: Sad Mona Lisa Lisa.

La folie et l'horreur, froides et taciturnes.

Gilbert O'Sullivan ft. Thin Lizzy: Himself.

Without a leader, green ants are confused.

10 extravagant lives that serve no purpose.

Bison herd protection in the New Digital Age.

Alors chouchou, t'y vas au bled voir les singes?

The Origin of Life: Five questions worth asking.

Ma pauvre muse, hélas ! Qu'as-tu donc ce matin?

McDonald Trump's Defect Drive-Inn Piscinema.

You can't be in Heaven if you know others are in Hell.

Young kids shouldn't be watching porn, simply simple.

A man's wealth may be superior to him. ~ Cameroon proverb.

Humanity will of course use virtuality for its worst fantasies.

Great Spirit, let me realize You are in charge. I'm to do what You want.

When the demon is at your door, in the morning it won't be there no more!

See You On The Bill Laswellas Marquesas Islands, you Millennials of the world!

If the cockroach wants to rule over the chicken, it must hire the fox as a bodyguard.

Play to loose.

Houdini you do?

Merci et à bientôt.

And the ship sails on.

Good is good enough.

The show must go on.

Nature versus virtuality.

Einstein was not a banker.

Best before the end of the world.

Slowly going the way of the buffalo.

And if you just put your hands in mine...

Making love to my PC with a monkey on my knee.

Here's some ideas for a drawing, let's have a Menaissance!

USAXIOMERICANADADA: Various: Trance Europe Express.

Searching For The Young American Soul Rebels, like Barron Trump!

Oh I'll Be Free, just like that bluebird, Oh I'll Be Free, ain't that just like me.

Come on!

Get a room U2!

The Will To Live.

Not my ancestor.

Expulsion of Self.

In Good We Trust.

Lies have long legs.

Like a bird in flight.

Race and Unreason.

In Groove We Trust.

Preacher Preacher!...

The Right To Paradox.

Shuffling into the Light.

So here it is for all to see...

Trump: Prophet of Deceit.

Webpage has gone extinct.

Say more than no to racism.

Back to Life, Back to Reality.

They call me the hyacinth girl.

A sexual Ice-Age is coming on.

High Hair for Helmut Newton.

There's no farting like abfahrting.

21st Century Ronald Lainglaufing.

Thank You For Flying Middle Class.

In reverse regret I salute u, dear reader.

Mon shambabble, my freezer, my dweller!

Change the world with your own two hands.

Hey La, Hey La Lo La, Hey La, Hey La Lo La.

The world's in a psychosis these days – in our time.

Reach the beach... of each... echo beach... each beach...

All these phrases are in fact polaroids of a fading world.

There's a crack in everything, that's how the Light gets in.

And it seems to you I lived my life like a bison in the wind....

When you get to where you wanna be, don't even mention it!

Climate Change ain't happening folks, it just ain't happening.

62 people have as much money as 3.5 billion people on this planet.

We must fill our eyes and ears with things that are the beginning of a great dream.

If You Just Put Your Hands In Mine, We're Gonna Leave All Our Troubles Behind.

Sarah Smiles: 1 l. Chandon Brut Classic, 2 l. Alaskan Grizzly Bear urine, sulphuric acids.

No more.

What's next?

Off Da Hook.

Over and out.

Aux Marquises.

Please no more.

Get up stand up.

A world of light...

Life is the answer.

Loving Nick Cave.

Consider me gone.

Bring me a horizon.

Watch me fall apart.

Blue Funk Is A Fact.

Chic: At last I'm free.

Goodbye, my friends!

Like a thief in the night.

Free at last! Free at last?

Adieu, Adieu, All's Vanity.

All at sea in clear blue water.

RIP Michael Soft Mon Amour.

I'm transforming, I'm vibrating.

Until after the buffalo was gone.

2016 Out of the Dark Part 1-2-3.

... I just love to watch them roll...

Here in this life until we are done.

When we wake up in World War E.

Don't let the sun set in your own skull.

What the world needs is a shift of stars.

To the land where the green ants dream.

We're Gonna Walk And Don't Look Back!

We travel on the quiet road... the overload.

However long the night, the dawn will break.

Comandante Jimi Hendrix: Rays Of The New Sun.

The Internet is the Dawn of Man, we finally have arrived.

What doesn't kill you makes you stronger, what does kill you makes you invincible.

Unplug, Kick Back, Relax and Enjoy Your: Freedom!

www.ingramcontent.com/pod-product-compliance
Lightning Source LLC
Chambersburg PA
CBHW020238130626
46549CB00005B/1958